STREAMS
IN THE DESERT
SAMPLER

Other books by **Mrs. Charles** E. Cowman:

Streams in the Desert
Streams in the Desert, Volume 2
Springs in the Valley
        also published as Streams, Vol. 3
Traveling Toward Sunrises
        also published as Streams, Vol. 4
Words of Comfort and Cheer
        also publihed as Streams, Vol. 5
Mountain Trailwlays for Youth:
        Devotions for Young People

STREAMS
IN THE DESERT
⁘ SAMPLER ⁘

Mrs. Charles E. Cowman

Daybreak Books

Zondervan Publishing House
Grand Rapids, Michigan

STREAMS IN THE DESERT SAMPLER
Copyright © 1983 by The Zondervan Corporation
Grand Rapids, Michigan

Daybreak Books are published by the Zondervan
Publishing House, 1415 Lake Drive, S.E.,
Grand Rapids, Michigan 49506

Library of Congress Cataloging in Publication Data

Streams in the desert. Selections.
    Streams in the desert sampler.
    "Compiled from Streams in the desert and Streams in the
desert, vol. 2" — P.
    1. Devotional calendars. I. Cowman, Charles E., Mrs., 1870-
1960. II. Title.
BV4810.S8425 1983   242'.2   83-12501
ISBN 0-310-37651-3

All Scripture quotations, unless otherwise noted, are taken from
the HOLY BIBLE: NEW INTERNATIONAL VERSION (North
American Edition). Copyright © 1973, 1978, 1984, by The
International Bible Society. Used by permission of Zondervan
Bible Publishers.

Compiled from *Streams in the Desert; Streams in the Desert,
Volume 2;* and new material.

Compiled and edited by Julie Ackerman Link
Designed by Martha Bentley

Cross-stitch patterns for designs used on cover are available from
Leisure Arts, P.O. Box 5595, Little Rock, AR 72215.

Printed in the United States of America

86 87 88 89 90 91 92 / 10 9 8 7 6 5

FOREWORD

A recurring theme throughout the writings of Mrs. Charles
E. Cowman, one of the world's most popular devotional writers, is that the seasons of the Christian life
often follow a pattern similar to the seasons of the year.

Spring, the season of new life, is a time for celebrating the
resurrection of all nature as well as the resurrection of our
Savior—God's proof that He can and will raise us above
even the most hopeless circumstances.

Summer, the season of growing, is also a time of violent
storms. So it is for Christians. The fierce wind and driving
rain of adversity are not pleasant, but they are necessary for
us to grow strong in our faith.

Fall, the season of change, is a time Christians must exercise their faith for the future. The harvest has ended and the
prospect of a long winter is discouraging. But just as we can
look back to God's protection and purpose in summer's
storms, we can look forward, in faith and with great anticipa-
tion, to God's provision throughout the winter.

Winter, the season in nature often associated with death, is
a time of waiting for the Christian. During the times we feel
useless and abandoned by God, we must wait on Him for the
miraculous resurrection of springtime.

Streams in the Desert Sampler is a compilation of more
than one hundred of Mrs. Cowman's devotionals on these
themes.

The Publisher

Part 1

Spring

He draws up
   the drops of water,
  which distill as rain
    to the streams;
the clouds pour down
   their moisture
  and abundant showers
    fall on mankind.

Job 36:27–28

Sorrowful, yet always rejoicing (2 Cor. 6:10).

Sorrow was beautiful, but her beauty was the beauty of the moonlight shining through the leafy branches of the trees in the wood, and making little pools of silver here and there on the soft green moss below.

When Sorrow sang, her notes were like the low sweet call of the nightingale, and in her eyes was the unexpectant gaze of one who has ceased to look for coming gladness. She could weep in tender sympathy with those who weep, but to rejoice with those who rejoice was unknown to her.

Joy was beautiful, too, but his was the radiant beauty of the summer morning. His eyes still held the glad laughter of childhood, and his hair had the glint of the sunshine's kiss. When Joy sang his voice soared upward as the lark's, and his step was the step of a conqueror who has never known defeat. He could rejoice with all who rejoice, but to weep with those who weep was unknown to him.

"But we can never be united," said Sorrow wistfully.

"No, never." And Joy's eyes shadowed as he spoke. *"My* path lies through the sunlit meadows, the sweetest roses bloom for my gathering, and the blackbirds and thrushes await my coming to pour forth their most joyous lays."

"My path," said Sorrow, turning slowly away, "leads through the darkening woods, with moon-flowers only shall my hands be filled. Yet the sweetest of all earth-songs— the love song of the night—shall be mine; farewell, Joy, farewell."

Even as she spoke they became conscious of a form standing beside them; dimly seen, but of a Kingly Presence, and a great and holy awe stole over them as they sank on their knees before Him.

"I see Him as the King of Joy," whispered Sorrow, "for on His Head are many crowns, and the nailprints in His hands and feet are the scars of a great victory. Before Him all my sorrow is melting away into deathless love and gladness, and I give myself to Him forever."

"Nay, Sorrow," said Joy softly, "but *I see* Him as the King of Sorrow, and the crown on His head is a crown of thorns, and the nailprints in His hands and feet are the scars of a great agony. I, too, give myself to Him forever, for sorrow with Him must be sweeter than any joy that I have known."

"Then we are *one* in Him," they cried in gladness, "for none but He could unite Joy and Sorrow."

Hand in hand they passed out into the world to follow Him through storm and sunshine, in the bleakness of winter cold and the warmth of summer gladness, "as sorrowful yet always rejoicing."

> Should Sorrow lay her hand upon thy shoulder,
>   And walk with thee in silence on life's way,
> While Joy, thy bright companion once, grown colder,
>   Becomes to thee more distant day by day?
> Shrink not from the companionship of Sorrow,
>   She is the messenger of God to thee:
> And thou wilt thank Him in His great tomorrow—
>   For what thou knowest not now, thou then shalt see;
> She is God's angel, clad in weeds of night,
> With "whom we walk by faith and not by sight."

When you walk, your steps will not be hampered; when you run, you will not stumble (Prov. 4:12).

The Lord will guide you always (Isa. 58:11).

A father and his son were camped in a wooded area a little ways from the nearest village. The father had a letter which needed mailing and asked his son to take it to the post office in the village. The father took his son to the edge of camp and showed him the trail which led to the village. "But Father," said the little boy, "I don't see how that path will ever reach town." The father took his hand in his and pointed, explaining, "See down the trail to that big tree where the trail seems to come to an end?" "Oh, yes, sir, I see that the path goes that far; but the village is not there!" "Well, when you get to that big tree, you will see further on around the bend and down the trail. Just go to the tree and then follow the trail until you come to the next corner, then look ahead and follow it some more until you see some houses. When you come to the houses, you will see the post office. There you can mail my letter!"

> I know not when or where I go from this familiar scene;
> But He is here and He is there, and all the way between.
> And when I pass from all I know, to that dim, vast unknown,
> Though late I stay or soon I go, I shall not go alone.

> —Selected

The love of God quite as often withholds the view of the entire distance of the winding path through life. He reveals it to us step by step and from corner to corner. Hence it is necessary to trust Him to lead, for He can see around the bend in the road. He knows what lies ahead, and whether we can cope with the situation now or later. He consults our wants, not our wishes, like a wise and loving Father. His corners are not the end of the way. Corners discipline faith, teach us patience to walk step by step, and fit us for blessing. Because our vision is limited, it causes us to continually seek His guidance.

DAY THREE

The Lord will guide you always; he will satisfy your needs in a sun-scorched land and will strengthen your frame. You will be like a well-watered garden, like a spring whose waters never fail (Isa. 58:11).

The children playing in the garden wanted to pick a flower for their mother. With lack of wisdom, but loving hearts, they pulled a large bud, enfolded in green, velvety leaves. Poor bud, untimely plucked from its parent stem, never to unfold as a thing of beauty, only left to wither and die! God's flowers are always wisely pulled. He wants the buds as well as the blossoms, but He guides His hands wittingly. He makes no mistakes. That lovely flower, as dear to you as life itself, is not left to wither and die. It is but transplanted to a sunnier land, to the King's own palace garden.

Be still, and know that I am God (Ps. 46:10).

In this modern day everything is performed with urgency. Efficiency experts are called in to perfect operations so the result will be speedier production. If a business does not have the latest technological apparatus, it is in danger of being "lost in the dust" of advancement.

Speed also has its disadvantages. The world seems smaller and less spectacular when you realize how few hours it takes to span the oceans and circle the globe. The wonder at the beauty along the wayside is transferred to the awesomeness at the genius of man to create the marvelous machines that whirl past us at enormous speeds. Can you wonder that modern life today is such a strain? Do you ever reflect upon the quietness in nature? Off into the hills, away from the busy thoroughfares of life, there is a stillness that is pulsating with growing things. The forests and fields are with quiet patience absorbing the warmth of sun and drops of rain.

Have you ever thought how pleasant is the voice of God? It is to be compared with the refreshing sound of running water in a pebbly brook—musical, delightfully gentle, humble. His command of "stand still" is to slow us down to a more moderate pace. We can then see His signs along the way.

DAY FIVE

Forgetting what is behind . . . I press on toward the goal (Phil. 3:13–14).

One of God's glorious gifts to mankind is to bestow upon him new opportunities and new challenges. A chance to try again, to make another endeavor to successfully accomplish the ambitions which were perhaps cast aside with discouragement in the past. Life is full of beginnings. As one stands at the gate and with doubtful hand draws aside the curtain and peers into the unknown, he begins today by taking his first step across a new threshold. It is already beautiful because it is from our Lord.

Gazing at the far horizons and half wondering what the future will bring, pause but a moment to reflect over the old volume of time now past. The pages may have been marred by mistakes and torn by intentions, but a few more miles have been covered on the upward climb, pressing toward the mark.

> Through many dangers, toils and snares
>   We have already come,
> 'Twas grace that brought us safe thus far,
>   And grace will lead us Home.

It has not been our own achievement. Great has been our Father's faithfulness; new every morning have been His mercies. He faileth never!

For whoever wants to save his life will lose it, but whoever loses his life for me will find it (Matt. 16:25).

The following parable brings home the truth of our Master's words:

There are two seas in Palestine. One is fresh and there are fish in it. Slashes of green adorn its banks. Trees spread their branches over it, and stretch out their thirsty roots to sip of healing water. Along its shores the children play as children played when He was there. He loved it. He could look across its silvery surface when He spoke His parables. And on a rolling plain not far away He fed the five thousand people.

The River Jordan flows on South into another sea. Here is no splash of fish, no fluttering leaf, no song of birds, no children's laughter. Travelers choose another route, unless on urgent business. The air hangs heavy above its waters, and neither man, nor beast, nor fowl will drink.

What makes this mighty difference in these neighbor seas? Not the River Jordan. It empties the same good water into both. Not the soil on which they lie. Not the country round about.

This is the difference. The Sea of Galilee receives but does not keep the Jordan. For every drop that flows into it, another drop flows out. The giving and receiving go on in equal measure.

The other sea is shrewder, hoarding its income jealously. It will not be tempted into generous impulse. Every drop it gets, it keeps.

The Sea of Galilee gives and lives. The other sea gives nothing. It is named the Dead Sea.

There are two kinds of people in the world.

There are two seas in Palestine.

Only the persons who continue full of life are like the Sea of Galilee, which gives and lives!

Can you fathom the mysteries of God? . . . If only I knew where to find him. . . . My ears had heard of you but now my eyes have seen you (Job 11:7; 23:3; 42:5).

ccording to Tennyson's lines it is a very simple thing to find God. He is near at hand; speak to Him! Would that it were as easy as that. But for most of us the reality and nearness of God is a "discovery."

An illustration of this "discovery" is found in the Book of Job. It is the cry of a baffled man who finds his inherited religion insufficient. He cried, "If only I knew where to find him."

Then follows the everlasting quest; and the great "discovery": "My ears had heard of you but now my eyes have seen you." Oh, it is a monumental moment in any life when the eyes of the spirit come open and "hearsay" religion gives place to the first hand experience of the Presence.

After the "discovery" and after the first hand experience, Spurgeon makes this admonition: "A Christian should be a striking likeness of Jesus Christ. You have read lives of Christ, beautifully and eloquently written, but the best life of Christ is His living biography, written out in the words and actions of His people. If we were what we profess to be, and what we should be, we would be pictures of Christ; yea, such striking likenesses of Him that the world would not have to hold us up by the hour together, and say, "Well, it seems somewhat of a likeness": but they would, when they once beheld us, exclaim, "He has been with Jesus; he has been taught of Him; he is like Him; he has caught the very idea of the holy Man of Nazareth, and he works it out in his life and every day actions."

> Speak to Him, thou, for He hears, and
> Spirit with Spirit shall meet—
> Closer is He than breathing, and
> Nearer than hands and feet.
> —Tennyson

Until now you have not asked for anything in my name. Ask and you will receive, and your joy will be complete (John 16:24).

Beware in your prayers of limiting God, not only by unbelief, but by fancying that you know what He can do. Expect things above all that you ask or think. "The Lord can give you much more than that" (2 Chron. 25:9).

God gives His children the liberty to ask whatever they will because through growth in Christ they have reached a position of intelligent responsibility in His kingdom. He recognizes the fact that one attains this wisdom and He honors the asking aright. "Ask whatever you wish, and it will be given you" (John 15:7).

Alexander the Great had a famous, but indigent, philosopher in his court. The adept man of science was once particularly hard-up financially. To whom alone should he apply but to his patron, the conqueror of the world? His request was no sooner made than granted. Alexander gave him a commission to receive of his treasury whatever he wanted. He immediately demanded in his sovereign's name ten thousand pounds. The treasurer, surprised at so large a demand, refused to comply, but waited upon the king and represented to him the affair, adding withal how unreasonable he thought the petition and how exorbitant the sum. Alexander listened with patience, but as soon as he heard the remonstrance replied, "Let the money be instantly paid. I am delighted with this philosopher's way of thinking; he had done me a singular honor: by the largeness of his request he shows the high idea he has conceived, both of my superior wealth and my royal munificence."

Thus let us honor what the inspired writer expresses as the marvelous loving-kindness of Jehovah: "He that spared not His own Son, but delivered Him up for us all, how shall He not with Him freely give us all things?"

You are the light of the world. . . . let your light shine before men . . . (Matt. 5:14, 16).

Twenty-two planes from a naval air station were aloft at dusk participating in maneuvers when the fog swept in unexpectedly. Eight of them raced immediately to landing fields, but the others were caught in a swiftly forming impenetrable blanket. Four planes crashed, one of them bursting into flames, as twelve pilots dived blindly through the fog. Two hours later only two planes were aloft. Suddenly there went out over the radio this message, "All automobile owners go to the field outside the city. Two fliers are lost in the fog and you are going to help them to land." Soon the roads approaching the field were crowded with cars creeping through the inky blackness, hardly able to see with their feeble lights. As the cars arrived the authorities lined them up with the cars facing inward around the field. More than twenty-five hundred completely surrounded the landing strip. The word was passed around, "All lights on!" The lights on no single car made much impression upon that night and fog, but the lights of two-thousand five hundred of them lighted the field so brightly that a transport pilot could go aloft and guide the two aviators down to safety.

Neither your light nor mine is very bright, but if each and all would focus the light we have upon this world with its fog of sin and distress, then it would be so bright that our Master Pilot, Christ, could go aloft and bring every lost soul to a safe landing.

For it is God who works in you both to will and to act according to his good purpose (Phil. 2:13).

We are told that the shivering weeds of the Arctic regions are nothing less than our forest trees—the stately oak and the sturdy elm. The very grasses and ferns of the temperate climate become trees in the tropics.

Who knows of what development we are capable when we find ourselves lifted from the dreary realm of our coldness and doubt to dwell in the summer of God's presence? How often have men and women without special genius or great gifts risen up into resistless power for God by the indwelling might of His Spirit? It is not only the reception of a germ of new life that is promised; it is a change of soil, of atmosphere, of condition.

If God can paint the blush on the bud which hangs from the limb of the rose, and make the dew-drops of morning tremble like diamonds on the virgin-white lip of the lily; if He can plant the rivers in lines of rippling silver, and can cover His valley floor with carpets of softest green, tacked down with lovely daisies and laughing daffodils; if He can scoop out the basin of the seven seas and pile up the rugged granite of the mountains until they pierce the turquoise skies; if He can send a Niagara thundering on a mighty and majestic minstrelsy from century to century; if He can fuel and refuel the red-throated furnace of a million suns to blaze His universe with light; if on the lovely looms of heaven, He can weave the delicate tapestry of a rainbow, and at eventide fashion a fleece of crimson to curtain the setting sun, and across the black bosom of the night that follows bind a glittering girdle spangled with ten thousand stellar jewels; then we cannot doubt His willingness to provide for us, His children, fathomless oceans of spiritual power which are ours "to receive" as we walk daily in glad obedience to His voice. The power of God through His Spirit will work within us to the degree that we permit it. The choice is ours.

DAY ELEVEN

If anything is excellent or praiseworthy—think about such things (Phil. 4:8).

It is not what one does, nor is it what one says, but it is what one thinks that makes the man. What one thinks determines what he will say and do. A person may try to make his words and actions to be much different than he actually thinks, but it will be all in vain. For it is still the thoughts that manage to break through the actions and the words regardless how closely they are guarded. Others can always see the soul when it is off guard.

Paul knew the human mind and character very well. He suggested that we are to think on all things that are true, noble, right, pure, lovely, and admirable; and as these are allowed to dwell in our thoughts they cannot help but transform us into their likeness.

Do not weary of the training that is in store for you. To be the person you most desire will take a very large part of your Christian life. Do not tire of trying the good thoughts, putting aside the bad. When you are about to give up in despair, the Holy Spirit is willing to live those thoughts through you. Give Him the opportunity to do the work which He was placed in your life to do.

The Lord will guide you always (Isa. 58:11).

He makes my feet like the feet of a deer, he enables me to go on the heights (Hab. 3:19).

Advance into each new experience on your knees. Faith does not concern itself with the entire journey. That first step is all that is needed. Breathe a prayer for courage to fill your legs as well as your heart as you face the unknown, the unexpected. Put your hand into the hand of God. He gives the calmness and serenity of heart and soul. As He endures, you too can endure the climb over sharp rocks and crags. Climb with Him to the end—yea, even to the end of life's trail. "The peak that is nearest the storm-cloud is nearer the stars of light." He gives the courage for which you pray to rise above the valley. Heed the Master's voice and press bravely on to the fulfillment of your task. You have a whole lifetime to scale.

> A Voice said, "CLIMB." And he said, "How shall I climb?
> The mountains are so steep that I cannot climb."
> The Voice said, "CLIMB OR DIE."
> He said, "But how? I see no way up those steep ascents.
> This that is asked of me is too hard for me."
>> The Voice said, "CLIMB or PERISH, soul and body of thee,
>> mind and spirit of thee. There is no second choice for
>> any son of man. CLIMB or DIE."

Some of the bravest mountaineers have related incredible tales concerning their climbs up the hills of earth. Sometimes they were aware of the presence of a Companion who was not among the earthly party of climbers on the mountains.

How much more positive is the presence of the Heavenly Guide as God's mountaineers climb the high places of the Spirit!

God's mountain climbers are created to walk in precarious places, not on the easy levels of life.

Do not limit the Limitless God! With Him face the new trail and follow on unafraid, for you walk not alone!

DAY THIRTEEN

But there is a God in heaven who reveals mysteries (Dan. 2:28).

Whenever your adversary pours in upon you like a flood suggesting all kinds of impossibilities and improbabilities, what are you to do and how are you to go forward? Take down the old Book; sit far into the night; read the promises and the prophecies. Read again the heart-warming words of Daniel: "There is a God in heaven who reveals mysteries." Your night will unveil new stars never seen by day. On the black thunder-cloud a rainbow will appear—God's everlasting covenant—and you will find a sunrise at midnight.

> "There's acres of blue up there," he said,
>   "Beyond all these clouds and rain;
> There's oceans of joy and love somewhere;
>   Apart from sorrow and pain."
>
> "There's millions of stars that man's never seen
>   Where life can begin anew;
> There's perfect calm where the ends of a rainbow
>   Dip into acres of blue."   —Selected

What shall you do? Act as people who have no faith, no light, no discernment? You cannot be like the unbelievers caught in the whirlpool and sink beneath the swirling waters of doubt and despair. You are a pilgrim of the day; a pilgrim of the light, guided by a glow as soft and tender as it is warm and luminous. Thank God for the assurance of Divine guidance, and pray that you may stand in the right relationship to all the impossibilities and improbabilities.

Trust in the dark brings Triumph at dawn.

The harvest truly is plentiful, but the workers are few (Matt. 9:37).

Tragedy had struck at the very heart of the British Empire —one of her favorite sons lay still in death. The Duke of Wellington, once invincible in battle, now lay lifeless in the great hall, surrounded only by those vigilant sentries who maintained their final watch.

Dignitaries journeyed from every dominion and protectorate to pay tribute to their fallen hero and statesman, and a special section was established in the great cathedral for the chosen representative of every military unit of the vast colonial army—every regiment of every country flying the Union Jack would stand in final homage to their great leader.

One of the greatest imperatives of the Gospel rings with undisguised urgency as it expresses the supreme wish of the Saviour to be represented in His great Kingdom by members of every tribe and nation. The Master gave vivid expression of this burning desire as He stood on the verdant mountain, high above glimmering Galilee, and spoke the words that have dominated Christian thought for centuries. "Go ye therefore and teach all nations. . . ."

A cry from the heart of black slaves reached the throne of God. Dark Africa stretched forth her dusky hands beseeching Him for help. God heard, but to answer their cry for help He needed a human voice. An angel could not carry to the black man the sweet story of the matchless love of God. A young Scotchman sat at his loom weaving—he heard a faint cry—a cry of pain. He heard it in the stillness of the night; he heard it through the cacophonies of day-time city life. Should he leave home and friends to bury himself amid Africa's wilds? The whole wide world knows the answer, for David Livingstone gave of himself on Africa's soil. The harvest of his life may be seen in the countless multitude of Africa's sons and daughters who have been "transformed into His likeness."

The Lord of the harvest wanted to sow a great field with living seeds in age-old China. He needed a sower. One Sunday morning He found Hudson Taylor walking by the seashore. He spoke to him saying, "If you will let Me, I will walk all over China through you." On that day of days a grain of wheat fell into the ground and died. Multiplied thousands of living grains are the result.

Very early on the first day of the week, just after sunrise, they were on their way to the tomb . . . (Mark 16:2).

This little group of Christ's devoted followers, who had trudged along with the jeering, taunting mob up the steep hill to the place called Calvary, were on their way to the tomb "just after sunrise." Just a few hours before they had seen Christ's enemies nail His precious body to an old wooden cross, and He had been left there to die on the hill lone and gray outside the city wall of old Jerusalem. How bleeding and broken were their hearts! How crushed their spirits! Suddenly all their lights had gone out and their future hopes had been snapped, as it were in twain. When hope is gone, the last hope, desperate despair invariably follows.

Had He not told them that He would rise again! Had He not said to Mary and Martha, "I am the Resurrection and the Life"? And had He not raised Lazarus after he had been dead four days! How easily His precious words are forgotten when we are plunged into a night of thick darkness, an hour of naked faith, and we cannot see our Father's hand or discern His presence! We fail to remember that "In the pitch-black night when there's no outer light, it is the time for faith to shine."

What wondrous surprises awaited these weary-hearted, bewildered followers! They were greeted by angels! They heard them make the announcement, and it was made exclusively to them: "He is not here: for He is risen as He said!" What rest is brought to them! It whispered peace! Sweet peace! Their bitter night of weeping now ended in a morning of joy! "Never the exquisite pain, then never the exquisite bliss." Oh, the gladness, the shouts of triumph on that first Easter morn! The morning time of all the ages! Christ's triumph over Satan! It reaches down the ages and touches our own hearts at this very hour. We triumph in His resurrection victory! Forever is Satan a defeated foe!

DAY SIXTEEN

He showed himself to these men and gave many convincing proofs that he was alive. He appeared to them over a period of forty days and spoke about the kingdom of God (Acts 1:3).

Easter season—spring—the lovely time of the year when we commemorate the glorious conquest of our RISEN LORD! How wondrously beautiful it is in each opening spring, after the bleak winter months, when the time of the singing of birds is come and God's miracle touch is seen on every tree, leaf, and flower, and all things are waking into new life—that we take into our hearts afresh the blessed fact of *our Lord's resurrection!*

What wondrous things occurred during the forty days, when to His own *He showed Himself alive!* How their hearts must have burned within them when He opened the Scriptures, and to them was given the revelation of the LIVING CHRIST! How natural, how easy were His manifestations! How noiseless the footsteps of Omnipotence! He joined the two downcast disciples on the Emmaus road on the Sabbath afternoon, and when He heard them saying, "We trusted that it had been He who would have redeemed Israel," He answered their doubts by a revelation of Himself! And that special revelation made them "witnesses of these things." What definite testimonies they bore ever afterwards! Oh, the glory of His Presence!

In every age a testimony has been left by people of every rank of having found themselves in awe and rapture in the radiant Presence! Abraham in the night, tending his altar fire; Moses on Sinai; Isaiah in the temple; Peter, James on the mount of Transfiguration, and John on the isle called Patmos! We too may know the shining Presence. "The living God is *among you*" (Josh. 3:10). "And surely I will be with you always, to the very end of the age" (Matt. 28:20).

Oh, that our eyes were opened that we might behold the riches of the glory of our inheritance, and the exceeding greatness of His power, which was wrought in Christ when God raised Him from the dead!

But he was pierced for our transgressions, he was crushed for our iniquities . . . and by his wounds we are healed (Isa. 53:5).

Dr. Alexander Macleod had a friend who was teaching a school in Jamaica. This teacher had made a rule that every one who told a lie in school should receive seven strokes on the palm with a strap. One day a little girl told a lie, and was called before the school to receive her punishment. She was a sensitive little thing, and the teacher was very sorry to strike her, but he must carry out the rule of the school. Her cry of pain when she received the first stroke went to his heart; he could not go on with her punishment. Yet he could not pass by her sin, and this is what he did. He looked over to the boys and asked, "Is there any boy who will bear the rest of her punishment?" And as soon as the words were spoken, up started a little fellow called Jim, who said, "Please, sir, I will!" And Jim went to the desk and received without a cry, the six remaining strokes.

Dr. Macleod tells the story, and adds: "And it was the vision of a Heart gentler still than that of this brave boy, but gentle with the same kind of gentleness, which filled the master's eyes with tears that day and made him close his books, and bring his scholars round about his desk, and tell them of the Gentle One, who long ago bore the punishment of us all." The story he told them is ours today.

"Carry each other's burdens, and in this way you will fulfill the law of Christ" (Gal. 6:2).

"No one is useless in the world who lightens the burden of it for anyone else."
—Charles Dickens

> Wounded for me, wounded for me,
> There on the cross He was wounded for me;
> Gone my transgressions, and now I am free,
> All because Jesus was wounded for me.
> —W. G. Ovens

DAY EIGHTEEN

They shall be abundantly satisfied with the fatness of thy house (Ps. 36:8 KJV).

Our world is one of vivid contrasts and fluent extremes.

What a contrast there is between the arid, lifeless, barren desert and the luxuriant oasis with its waving palms and its glorious verdure; between gaunt and hungry flocks and the herds that lie down in green pastures and beside the restful waters; between the viewless monotony of the shimmering plains and the mountain heights, resplendent in magnificent beauty.

What a difference there is between the aridity of an artificial, stinted existence—a desert existence—and the almost over-powering fruitfulness of a rich fertile valley, washed by gentle rains and bathed in filtered sunlight—the abundant life!

This lesson of contrasts finds its daily counterpart in the lives and experiences of Christian people. There are some who seem always to be kept alive on scant measure. Their spiritual garments are threadbare. Their existence is as barren and fruitless as the desert wastes. Life seems to have dried up, and purpose has so dehydrated that they wander aimlessly around the margins of life.

There are others who daily experience the inner peace and happiness that comes through a vigorous faith in the Saviour—a practical day-by-day faith that insures victory and "life more abundant." In a word, this is an experience that reaches out into the infinite as well as the eternal—sailing on the shoreless and fathomless seas of God and His unlimited grace. It is a life guaranteed to gratify the parched and arid soul.

When I tried to understand all this, it was oppressive to me till I entered the sanctuary of God (Ps. 73:16–17).

I n strange places and in unexpected ways God meets His own. Many times to one in deep soul distress there is a fresh revelation of the Divine presence. He brings the balm of healing. If one accepts the nail-pierced Hand, or a word from Him who whispers peace, all will be changed.

Two men were startled on the Emmaus Road when the Saviour overtook them. They were grieving because of His death. The crucifixion had been a tragic experience, too painful for them to bear. He stole softly to their side as they walked and talked. At His appearing the heavy weight was lifted from their troubled hearts.

They were on their way back to their nets, to take up their old occupation which was their livelihood three years before. At the dawn of day, after a night of despairing toil, they found a meal prepared for them by One who stood on the shore. The Lord Jesus Christ, with this tender touch, made Himself a living bright reality to them.

He still meets His own today in their hours of bitter disappointment; and such was the experience of one whose heart strings have been torn from the very roots. Bereavement had broken a loving home and life was like a tree that had been uprooted by a terrific tempest. While walking along the streets of a British city on the way to a Sunday service, a beautiful stone church was passed. On the bulletin board near the entrance were these words, "All ye who are weary, enter the sanctuary for quietness and prayer." The silent invitation was accepted. On one of the walls in the foyer of this great church something was written in Mosaic. It was a miniature sermon in vari-colored stones: "It was too hard for me until I went into the sanctuary of God: then understood I" (Ps. 73:16–17).

DAY TWENTY

. . . but be transformed by the renewing of your mind . . . (Rom. 12:2).

In the ditch there grows a briar, scratching, tearing. It sighs within itself and says, "Ah me, I cannot think what I was made for. I have no beauty and no worth. If only I were a bunch of violets on the bank, I might make somebody happy—but a briar! If I were but the oak tree whose branches come out so far and whose leaves make such sweet music as they rustle under the prodding of gentle breezes—then I would be of some good."

But now, here comes the gardener and digs up the briar by the roots and plants it in his garden. The briar is heard to mutter, "He doesn't know me or he wouldn't waste his time like this. He will never get any good out of me—a wretched briar covered with prickers!" But the gardener just laughs and says, "If I cannot get any good out of you, maybe I can put some good into you. We shall see."

Now, however, the briar was sadder than before. "It was bad enough living in the ditch, but to be among all of the sweet and dainty flowers and still be just a briar is just terrible. I knew I could never amount to anything!"

One day the gardener came and made a little slit, put a tiny bud in it and fastened it there. After a few weeks the little briar rose was aflame with color, and its fragrance was most exquisite. What a transformation! There was now little resemblance to the scraggly, bedraggled briar whose first home was in the ditch.

Our Heavenly Father is the husbandman. He understands the rough stock of our humanity. He knows its evil nature and its little worth, but He also knows how to put within it a new nature. Not of our struggling or strife does it come, for it is not from within that this grace must spring, but by our surrender to the divine Gardener—letting Him have His Way with us in everything. If we will permit Him to put into us what He desires, He can get out of us what He wills.

They will be like a well-watered garden, and they will sorrow no more (Jer. 31:12).

Down through the annals of time poets have compared rain to tears. They say "the heavens are weeping" when it rains. Jeremiah, one of the great Old Testament poets, compares the joyful soul to a watered garden. Being one of the most eloquent and wise among the many scribes, he expressed his innermost feelings in his description of the watered garden of the soul. It is like a garden on which there is falling an abundance of rain. Every plant stands erect with shining dignity. Each leaf glistens with fresh reviving. Each fragrant blossom displays its brightest hue. How lucid was Jeremiah. Rain does not shed tears, but pours forth resplendent beauty.

DAY TWENTY-TWO

"He will also send you rain for the seed you sow" (Isa. 30:23).

Ask the Lord for rain in the springtime; it is the Lord who makes the storm clouds (Zech. 10:1).

Sometimes it is hard to be joyous over rain. Is one glad for pain? Both can be sad disturbances in life. We often rebel within because of both. Who is the one who does not desire cloudless skies and painless bodies? The people who live in places of constant sunshine long for a few cloudy days. The joys of heaven will be magnified because of the memory of our clouded over-cast days here on earth.

In a life where perpetual springtime reigns there will be a watered garden of the soul—though it oft-times is watered by tears. It is the life closest to the "Man of Sorrows" who was Himself acquainted with grief that can bring blossoms of joy and peace. If His joy is in us, our joy is made full.

I am concerned for you and will look on you with favor; you will be plowed and sown (Ezek. 36:9).

God does not use the plow and harrow without intention! Where God plows He intends to sow! His plowing is proof He is for, and not against us! The husbandman is never so near the land as when he is plowing it: the very time when we are tempted to think that He hath forsaken us!

The plowman is a proof that he thinks you of value and worth cultivating—and He does not waste His plowing on the barren sand. He will not plow continually, but only for a time, and for a definite purpose. Soon He will close that process. "When a farmer plows for planting, does he plow continually?" (Isa. 28:24). Verily, no! Soon we shall, through these painful processes and by His gentle showers of grace, become His fruitful land. "The desolate land will be cultivated. . . . They will say, 'This land that was laid waste has become like the garden of Eden'" (Ezek. 36:34–35). And thus shall we be a praise unto Him.

"Someone must go through sore travail of soul before a life movement, outwardly visible, can be born," said Josephine Butler. The one who seeks release from the process of fruitage would expel the furrows from the face of Lincoln, and make St. Paul a mere esthetic—would rob the Divine Sufferer of His sanctity. We cannot have the result of the harvest without the process! The price must be paid.

> O God, wert Thou plowing
>   Thy profitless earth
> With the brave plow of Love,
> And the sharp plow of Pain?
>   But hark to the mirth
> Of wheatfield in harvest!
>   Dear Plower, well worth
> That plowing, this yellow-gold grain.
> —Unknown

Let the heavens rejoice, let the earth be glad; let the sea resound, and all that is in it; let the fields be jubilant, and everything in them. Then all the trees of the forest will sing for joy (Ps. 96:11–12).

There is a story of the Highlander of Scotland who every morning went out to a certain viewpoint near his cottage and stood with uncovered head. Asked if he prayed there, he said, "I come here every morning that I may take off my hat to the beauty of the world."

Of nature one has written, "God is speaking to us in the shimmering lake and placid river, in the mighty oak and tiny flower, in the lift of the mountain and in the surge of the sea. The world of nature, to the observing, responsive, and appreciative soul, is ever the garment of the Eternal."

Surely if the unbelieving astronomer is mad, so also must he be who seeks the order, the service and the beauty of the garden, the field, the valley and the mountain, and the river, but has found no God back of it all.

We believe not only that the rain "hath a father" but so also hath the rest of this blessed cosmos.

> Full many a gem of purest ray serene,
> The dark unfathomed caves of ocean bear;
> Full many a flower is born to blush unseen,
> And waste its sweetness on the desert air.
> —Gray's *Elegy*

"If a man is thirsty, let him come to me and drink . . ."(John 7:37).

A most unusual story is found in the first chapter of Judges. Achsah had received a gift of land from her father. As she surveyed her new holdings, she discovered, much to her consternation, that there were no water wells—the land was a barren waste.

Achsah sent word to her father Caleb that she would like to see him. She was called into his presence and was greeted with the question, "What can I do for you?" Her reply was definite. "Since you have given me land in the Negev, give me also springs of water." Her request was granted immediately. Caleb gave her the upper and lower springs.

Achsah might have been content with a dry, barren land, but how much better that she had the faith to say, "Give me a blessing."

No simpler, stronger symbol of the Spirit could be found than this, a Spring—a well-Spring—never dry—never turbid; from its clear depths, fed through the secret veins of earth, it gushes ever into life. It goes not downward, but it springs up and it flows out.

"All my fresh springs are in thee," said David. The soul that has found all its springs in God never knows its supply to fail or vary; we need both *upper and lower springs.* The Spirit of God in the highest regions of life and down to its lowest level—the need is still the same.

DAY TWENTY-SIX

But the land you are crossing the Jordan to take possession of is a land of mountains and valleys that drinks rain from heaven. It is a land the Lord your God cares for; the eyes of the Lord your God are continually on it from the beginning of the year to its end (Deut. 11:11–12).

Today, dear friends, we stand upon the verge of the unknown. There lies before us a new land and we are going forth to possess it. Who can tell what we shall find? What new experiences, what changes shall come, what new needs shall arise? But here is the cheering, comforting, gladdening message from our Heavenly Father, "It is a land the Lord your God cares for; the eyes of the Lord your God are continually on it from the beginning of the year to its end."

All our supply is to come from the Lord. Here are springs that shall never dry; here are fountains and streams that shall never be cut off. Here, anxious one, is the gracious pledge of the Heavenly Father. If He be the Source of our mercies they can never fail us. No heat, no drought can parch that river, "whose streams make glad the city of God" (Ps. 46:4).

The land is a land of *mountains* and *valleys*. It is not all smooth nor all down hill. If life were all one dead level the dull sameness would oppress us; we want the mountains and the valleys. The mountains collect the rain for a hundred fruitful valleys. Ah, so it is with us! It is the mountain difficulty that drives us to the throne of grace and brings down the shower of blessing; the mountains, the bleak mountains of life that we wonder at and perhaps grumble at, bring down the showers. How many have perished in the wilderness, buried under its golden sands, who would have lived and thriven in the mountain country; how many would have been killed by the frost, blighted with winds, swept desolate of tree and fruit but for the mountain—stern, hard, rugged, so steep to climb. God's mountains are a gracious protection for His people against their foes!

We cannot tell what loss and sorrow and trial are doing. Trust only. The Father comes near to take our hand and lead us on our way today. It shall be a good, a blessed journey!

You care for the land and water it; you enrich it abundantly. The streams of God are filled with water to provide the people with grain, for so you have ordained it. . . . The grasslands of the desert overflow; the hills are clothed with gladness (Ps. 65:9, 12).

Gladness! I like to cultivate the spirit of gladness! It puts the soul so in tune again, and keeps it in tune, so that Satan is shy of touching it—the chords of the soul become too warm, or too full of heavenly electricity, for his infernal fingers, and he goes off somewhere else! Satan is always very shy of meddling with me when my heart is full of gladness and joy in the Holy Ghost.

My plan is to shun the spirit of *sadness* as I would Satan; but, alas! I am not always successful. Like the devil himself it meets me on the highway of *usefulness,* looks me so fully in my face, till my poor soul changes color!

Sadness discolors everything; it leaves all objects *charmless;* it involves future prospects in darkness; it deprives the soul of all its aspirations, enchains all its powers, and produces a mental paralysis!

An *old believer* remarked, that *cheerfulness* in religion makes all its services come off with delight; and that we are never carried forward so swiftly in the ways of duty as when borne on the wings of *delight;* adding, that *Melancholy* clips such wings; or, to alter the figure, takes off our chariot wheels in duty, and makes them, like those of the Egyptians, drag heavily.

Therefore, as God's chosen people, holy and dearly loved, clothe yourselves with compassion, kindness, humility, gentleness and patience (Col. 3:12).

There is a story of an old man who carried a little can of oil with him everywhere he went, and if he passed through a door that squeaked, he poured a little oil on the hinges. If a gate was hard to open, he oiled the latch. And thus he passed through life lubricating all hard places and making it easier for those who came after him.

People called him eccentric, queer, and cranky; but the old man went steadily on refilling his can of oil when it became empty, and oiled the hard places he found.

There are many lives that creak and grate harshly as they live day by day. Nothing goes right with them. They need lubricating with the oil of gladness, gentleness, or thoughtfulness. Have you your own can of oil with you? Be ready with your oil of helpfulness in the early morning to the one nearest you. It may lubricate the whole day for him. The oil of good cheer to the downhearted one—Oh, how much it may mean! The word of courage to the despairing. Speak it.

Our lives touch others but once, perhaps, on the road of life; and then our ways diverge, never to meet again. The oil of kindness has worn the sharp, hard edges off of many a sin-hardened life and left it soft and pliable and ready for the redeeming grace of the Saviour.

A word spoken pleasantly is a large spot of sunshine on a sad heart. Therefore, "Give others the sunshine, tell Jesus the rest."

Commit to the Lord whatever you do, and your plans will succeed (Prov. 16:3).

It is life's largeness that most discourages earnest and conscientious souls. One thinks deeply of its meaning and responsibility. He is apt to be overwhelmed by the thought of its vastness. It has manifold relations toward God and toward man. Each of these relations has its binding duties. Every individual life must be lived amid countless antagonisms, and in the face of countless perils. Battles must be fought, trials encountered, and sorrows endured. One has to learn to commit his way unto the Lord. For every life has a divine mission to fulfill, a plan of God to work out. Then the brief earthly course is but the beginning of an endless existence, whose immortal destinies hinge upon fidelity in the present life. Looked at in this way, as a whole, there is something almost appalling in the thought of our responsibility in living.

When one thinks of life in this aspect, and sees it in its wholeness, he has not the courage to hope for success and victory, but stands staggered, well-nigh paralyzed, on the threshold. One should not view life in this manner. It does not come to us all in one piece. We do not get it even in years, but only in days—day by day. We look on before us, and as we count up the long years with their duties, struggles, and trials, the bulk is like a mountain which no mortal can carry; but we really never have more than one day's battles to fight, or one day's work to do, or one day's burdens to bear, or one day's sorrow to endure, in any one day. So commit just this one day unto Him. Commit . . .

> One day at a time. But a single day,
>   Whatever its load, whatever its length;
> And there's a bit of precious Scripture to say,
>   That according to each shall be our strength.
>   —Anonymous

Whoever is thirsty, let him come; and whoever wishes, let him take the free gift of the water of life (Rev. 22:17).

Of course if we do not thirst we will not care to come to the well and drink. Souls are dying all about us, not because there is no water near, but because they are not thirsty. Intense thirst is a pitiable condition; it is hopeless. The word "thirsty" describes the need that Christ is able to supply. It is not bodily thirst, but thirst of the soul, which He offers to quench. For the soul as well as the body has its thirsts, and there is no spring of earth at which they can be satisfied.

The words "let him come" show us the gate to the fountain flung wide open. There is no barrier in the way. We must leave our dry wastes, where no water is, and come to Christ.

Part 2

Summer

He fills his hands
    with lightning
  and commands it
    to strike its mark.
God's voice thunders
    in marvelous ways;
  he does great things
    beyond our understanding.
Job 36:32; 37:5

So keep up your courage, men, for I have faith in God . . . (Acts 27:25).

Paul's was a faith that triumphed in all sorts of conditions. It was in the midst of a storm that threatened complete destruction that he stood up before all and said, "I have faith in God." How much rough weather can your faith stand?

The disciples were very confident until the squall hit their boat. Then they did what the storm could not do; they awoke the Lord with their panic-inspired question, "Teacher, don't you care if we drown?" Of a different sort is the faith expressed in the forty-sixth Psalm: "God is our refuge and strength, an ever present help in trouble. Therefore we will not fear, though the earth give way and the mountains fall into the heart of the sea, though its waters roar and foam and the mountains quake with their surging."

John Newton has expressed the all-weather faith in one of his best hymns:

> Begone, unbelief, my Saviour is near,
> And for my relief will surely appear;
> By prayer let me wrestle, and He will perform;
> With Christ in the vessel, I smile at the storm.

DAY TWO

The eternal God is your refuge . . . (Deut. 33:27).

One night during a terrific storm a man walked along the shore of the sea. The clouds hung low overhead. The wind howled. Thunders roared. Lightning flashed and the rain poured down in torrents. The man pulled his overcoat closer around him, bent his body to the wind and hurried home. A little bird lost in the storm sought shelter under his coat; he took it in his hand, carried it home, placed it in a warm cage. The next morning after the storm had subsided, and the clouds had cleared away, he took the little bird to the door. It paused on his hand for a moment; then lifting its tiny wings, it hurried back to its forest home. Then it was that Charles Wesley caught the vision, and going back to his room he wrote the words to a song that is loved around the world today and will live on in time:

> Jesus, Lover of my soul
>   Let me to thy bosom fly,
> While the nearer waters roll,
>   While the tempest still is high:
>
> Hide me, O my Saviour, hide,
>   Till the storm of life be past;
> Safe into the haven guide,
>   O receive my soul at last!
>
> Other refuge have I none,
>   Hangs my helpless soul on thee;
> Leave, ah! leave me not alone,
>   Still support and comfort me.

He got up, rebuked the wind and said to the waves, "Quiet! Be still!" Then the wind died down and it was completely calm (Mark 4:39).

Several years ago while visiting certain of the Northern European countries, it was necessary for me to cross the North Sea in a large ocean liner. During the first days of the voyage we sped along over calm seas, but suddenly we were overtaken by a frightening tempest. The waves were like great mountains, and we were lifted to their heights. The great ship rocked and rolled, creaked and groaned. The faces of the passengers were blanched white with fear. Even the little ones clung to their mothers, sensing the nearness of danger—the very air was surcharged by an ominous foreboding of impending destruction. When it seemed that surely the ship had endured to the very limit, a man appeared on the scene. There was no trace of anxiety or concern on his face. His presence radiated calmness, rest and peace. With a voice full of gentleness he assured us, "all's well," and our fears disappeared.

Who was that man? The captain. He had taken that vessel through many a long voyage, plowed rough seas, met terrible storms, and had always arrived safely into port—flags of victory flying at top mast.

What have we to fear? Why do we look down? Where now is thy God? Is not our Captain on board, and with one word can He not say to the waves and winds, "Quiet! Be still!" and they obey Him? With hushed hearts let us listen for His sweet whisper of assurance, "All's well. It is I; be not afraid." With Christ in the vessel we smile at the storm.

Yes, one whose faith is continually stimulated by *the upward look* gives no ground to the attempted encroachment of despair. No matter how great the trouble or how dark the outlook, a quick lifting of the heart to God in a moment of real actual faith in Him will completely alter any situation and turn the darkness of midnight into glorious sunrise.

"Oh, that I had the wings of a dove! I would fly away and be at rest . . . I would hurry to my place of shelter, far from the tempest and storm" (Ps. 55:6, 8).

The sweetest songs of David were born in the storms of his life. This shepherd boy was ordained of God to wear the badge of honor as "earth's greatest songster." He found himself one day listening to the voice of the tempter and the Master-Musician had positioned him in the heart of a storm to teach him how to sing. But instead the Psalmist only muttered this moaning cry: "Oh, that I had the wings of a dove! I would fly away and be at rest . . . I would hurry to my place of shelter, far from the tempest and storm." Out from the fury of the storm rose loud notes of praise to his God on high. The result is two beautiful and melodious Psalms—23 and 91. These Psalms have comforted people of all generations. What would David have done with doves' wings? How far from the tempest would those frail pinions have carried him? How much the world would have lost without those comforting words from the struggling heart of "earth's greatest songster."

Be watchful of your pleas to the Throne of heaven when you are walking through storm-clouds of testing and physical exhaustion.

Turn to me and be gracious to me, for I am lonely and afflicted (Ps. 25:16).

A celebrated Scottish nobleman and statesman once replied to a correspondent that he was "plowing his lonely furrow."

Whenever God has required someone to do a big thing for Him, He often sends that individual to "plow a lonely furrow." He calls the person to go alone.

In the realm of suffering, the same is often also true. Just as David was "lonely and afflicted" so each of us may be called to suffer alone, as though there were no other being in the universe. Friends may sympathize with us or administer comfort or alleviation, but they enter not really into the experiences. In these we are alone. No one can meet your temptations for you, or fight your battles, or endure your trials. The tenderest of friendship, the holiest love, cannot enter into the solitariness in which each one of us lives apart.

DAY SIX

Let them sacrifice thank offerings and tell of his works with songs of joy (Ps. 107:22).

hat is a sacrifice? It is an offering to God. To "sacrifice thank offerings" is to praise God when you do not feel like it; when you are depressed and despondent; when your life is covered with thick clouds and midnight darkness. While we are admonished to "pray without ceasing," are we not also commanded to "rejoice evermore"?

Many homes display the motto, "Prayer Changes Things," and great blessing has resulted from this simple statement. We are all aware that prayer does change things. We know, also, that many times the enemy has not been moved one inch from his stronghold, although we have persisted in prayer for days, months—yes, often years.

Such was my own experience when passing through a time of very great pressure, and prayer did not change things. I came into possession of a wonderful secret. That secret is simply this: after we have prayed and believed, "Praise Changes Things."

The man who plants and the man who waters have one purpose, and each will be rewarded according to his own labor. For we are God's fellow workers . . . (1 Cor. 3:8–9).

One morning long before the Carpenter was to appear in His shop, the Carpenter's tools decided that they needed to have a conference to settle some of the problems that were steadily arising in their work. The first tool called to take the chair was Brother Hammer. The meeting informed him that he was to leave because he was too noisy with his work. "But," he said, "if I am to leave this carpenter shop, Brother Gimlet must go too; he is so insignificant that he makes very little impression."

Little Brother Gimlet rose to his feet and said, "All right, but Brother Screw must go also; you have to turn him around and around again and again to get him anywhere."

Brother Screw then said, "If you wish, I will go, but Brother Plane must leave as well; all his work is on the surface; there is no depth to it!"

To this, Brother Plane replied, "Well, Brother Rule will have to withdraw, if I do, for he is always measuring other folks as though he were the only one who is right!"

Brother Rule then complained against Brother Sandpaper, and said, "I just don't care, he is rougher than he ought to be, and he is always rubbing people the wrong way!"

In the midst of this discussion, the Carpenter of Nazareth walked in—earlier than they expected. He had come to perform His day's work. He first put on His apron and then went over to the bench to make a pulpit. He employed the screw, the gimlet, the sandpaper, the saw, the hammer, the plane, and all the other tools. After the day's work was over and the pulpit was finished, Brother Saw arose and said, "Brethren, I perceive that all of us are laborers together with God!"

Do there happen to be any people within your circle of acquaintances who do not perform their duties just the way you think they should? Perhaps it would be well to think twice before making any criticism or finding any fault with any one of God's instruments of service who is furthering His kingdom here on earth. If a selfish judgment were made against one of God's necessary tools and that tool was removed from his work, who would be the one causing God's work to be delayed?

The Lord is a refuge for the oppressed, a stronghold in times of trouble (Ps. 9:9).

well-known business man would drop into our office every few days. His visits were ever times of spiritual refreshing. His face was always wreathed in smiles. He had an elastic tread. He radiated victory. A few minutes in his presence and one felt the lifting tides of God, for victory acts as a contagion. The old prophets knew this secret when they wrote of the carpenter *encouraging* the goldsmith, and the goldsmith *encouraging* those that beat out the tongs, etc.

Recently this same man shuffled into our office, sank down in a chair, buried his face between his hands, and burst into tears. What had happened to this child of God? He had *fainted in the day of adversity.* He experienced a great calamity which swept away his home, his business, his money. Then he began to worry, and, in consequence, he lost his health and is now a physical wreck. Here was Satan's opportunity, and he was not slow to avail himself of it. He came with the insidious question. "How are you going to face the world?" He led this once triumphant Christian to the very edge of the precipice, and told him to cast himself down. Everything was dark, pitch dark.

The Father cares when He sees His children in a blinding storm, but He knows that faith grows in the tempest. He will hold our hands, bidding us not to try to *see* the next step we are to take. He who knows the paths of a hundred million stars, *knows the way* through the whirlwind and the storm, and has promised, "I will never, never let go your hand!"

There is a grave danger of many becoming *spiritually paralyzed* by depression. The forces of darkness are so imminent, the magnitude of the crisis is so great that many are being tempted to cry out with the disciples, "Lord, carest Thou not that we perish?" Yet He who may appear to be "asleep upon a pillow" is riding upon the storm in all His Divine majesty. The great need is for more faith in the omnipotent God.

DAY NINE

Even youths grow tired and weary, and young men stumble and fall; but those who hope in the Lord will renew their strength. They will soar on wings like eagles; they will run and not grow weary, they will walk and not be faint (Isa. 40:30–31).

Many are the lessons to be learned from the present chaotic world condition. We are taught the way of simple faith as we are driven back to the Word of God and prayer. We should make use of these adverse conditions! There is a lesson for us to learn from the eagle who sits on the edge of the precipice and watches the dark clouds overhead filling the sky with blackness. There he sits perfectly still, turning one eye and then the other towards the storm as the forked lightnings play back and forth. He never moves a feather until he feels the first burst of the breeze. It is then that he knows the hurricane has struck him. With a scream he swings his breast to the storm. It is the storm itself that he uses to soar upward into the black sky. God wants this experience to take place in the lives of every one of His children! He wants us to "soar on wings like eagles!" We can turn the storm clouds into a chariot!

A well-known man of God once made this statement: "My religious organs have been ailing for a while past. I have lain, a sheer hulk in consequence. But I got out my wings, and have taken a change of air." It is so often true—we do not use our wings! We walk along the road of life as mere pedestrians, and we tire so easily—for the ugliness of our circumstances burdens us down. In many different ways we can be put on the shelf or become bedridden—and "our religious organs are in danger of becoming sickly; of losing their brightness, both in mood and discernment."

We who keep too close to the road of life and do not respond to the Upward Calling, do not have time to breathe the lofty air of the heavenlies! But we who turn unto the Lord, the Omnipotent One, have the power of wings, and we rise from our tiresome journey into the higher heavens of the glories of our Most High God.

I tell you the truth, you will weep and mourn while the world rejoices. You will grieve, but your grief will turn to joy (John 16:20).

Sorrows are too precious to be wasted. That great man of God in a past generation, Alexander MacLaren of Manchester, used to bring out this overlooked truth. He reminded God's people that sorrows will, if we let them, "blow us to His breast, as a strong wind might sweep a man into some refuge from itself. I am sure there are many who can thankfully attest that they were brought nearer to God by some short, sharp sorrow than by long days of prosperity. Take care that you do not waste your sorrows; that you do not let the precious gifts of disappointment, pain, loss, loneliness, ill health, or similar afflictions that come into your daily life mar you instead of mending you. See that they send you nearer to God, and not that they drive you farther from Him."

Sorrows are God's winds, His contrary winds. Sometimes His strong winds. They are God's hurricanes. They take human life and lift it to higher levels and toward God's heavens. You have seen in the summer time a day when the atmosphere was oppressive. You could hardly breathe it was so unbearable. But when a cloud appeared on the horizon and grew larger and then threw out that blessing for the world, the storm rose, lightning flashed and thunder pealed. The storm covered the world and immediately the atmosphere was cleaned; new life was in the air and the world was changed. Human life is worked out according to exactly the same principle, and when the storm breaks the atmosphere is changed, clarified, filled with new life and a part of heaven is brought down to earth.

DAY ELEVEN

You have filled my heart with greater joy . . . (Ps. 4:7).
A happy heart makes the face cheerful . . . (Prov. 15:13).

It would be foolish to think that all who smile are happy. There are "smiles" and "smiles"—smiles self-conscious, smiles self-complacent, smiles conceited, smiles sarcastic, smiles superficial, smiles satanic, smiles cynical, smiles critical, smiles occasional, smiles habitual, smiles spiritual. There are smiles good, smiles better, and smiles best. Each sort has its own peculiar value. It is the "best" sort of smiles we advocate. The "best" sort go deepest, last longest, and accomplish most good.

The best kind of smiles are not "put on." They "come out" because they are "in." They are the result of a satisfied, thankful, and glad heart. They are the exterior expression of an interior joy, which glows and grows as the days go by.

It is the satisfied and restful heart that makes a radiant face. When we are contented at the center, the countenance will be calmly cheerful. When the spirit is satisfied and glad, the glory is expressed in look and touch and tone.

Christ is the secret, the source, the substance, the center, and the circumference of all true and lasting gladness.

I had a friendly smile, I gave that smile away.
The postman and the milkman seemed glad of it each day.
I gave my smile away as happy as could be.
And every time I gave it, my smile came back to me.

Smile a smile!
While you smile
Another smiles,
And soon there are miles
And miles of smiles,
And life's worth while
If you but smile.
—Anonymous

54

Don't you know that when you offer yourselves to someone to obey him as slaves, you are slaves to the one whom you obey—whether you are slaves to sin, which leads to death, or to obedience, which leads to righteousness? (Rom. 6:16).

It was a dark and stormy night. Most of the sheep had come back to the fold, but three were missing. The faithful watchdog was lying in the corner of her kennel with her young and thought her toils were over for the day. Suddenly the shepherd called her, and pointing to the flock cried: "Three are missing, go." She gave a sad look at her little ones, and then a look of obedient love at her master, and off into the darkness she plunged. Back she came after an hour with two of the sheep. There was blood upon her and upon them. Hard she had fought for their lives with the thorns and torrents, but they were saved. With a grateful look she threw herself down in the kennel and gathered her brood to her bosom once more.

But once again the master called, with his stern but kind voice, and pointing to the wilderness, said: "One is still lost, go." She looked up in his face with unutterable longing, but he still pointed to the wilderness. Into the darkness she plunged once more. Late in the night a feeble scratching was heard upon the door. The shepherd rose and opened it, and there she crouched half dead, and the poor wounded sheep was trembling by her side. She had found the lost one but it was at the cost of her very life. One look she gave into his face, which seemed to say, "I have loved you better than my life," and then she crawled over into her kennel and lay down with her little ones and grew still in death. She had loved her master and had given her life for his lost ones.

If a dog could love like that, with no eternity to reward her, no heaven to await her, only the smile of her master's approval in the last instant of her life, what should He not expect from us for whom He has given His life already, and to whom He wants to give a recompense that can never fade away? Shall we catch His glance as He looks out into the darkness and cries, "A thousand millions are lost, go"?

He persevered because he saw him who is invisible (Heb. 11:27).

Safety first has no place in God's missionary program. We are called upon to live dangerously. Oft in the silence of the night we seem to hear voices calling to us out from the past, voices of martyrs who loved not their lives unto death, martyrs who went joyfully to the stake singing His praises as the flames leaped about them; voices of those who laid down their lives during their servitude; voices of the pilgrims of the night, who with faces upturned toward the light which streamed down upon them from the Pearly White City as they marched bravely up the steep mountain sides to the place of death. "How long, O Lord," cry the martyrs who wait under the altar.

> They climbed the steep ascent to heaven,
> Through peril, toil or pain,
> Oh God, to us may grace be given
> To follow in their train!

They persevered because they saw Him who is invisible. What a challenge! Whose name will appear on the next roll of martyrs? "Let us encourage one another—and all the more as we see the Day approaching" (Heb. 10:25).

They are peering over the battlements on high, watching us as we run. Are they wondering if we are going to faint and fall out by the way—faint in this day of adversity? They have fought the good fight, kept the faith, and are wearing victors' crowns. They are looking into the face of Him whose visage was marred more than any man's. They followed Him up Calvary's hill, and now, He is looking upon them with love and is seeing of the travail of His soul, and is satisfied.

"They will feed beside the roads and find pasture on every barren hill" (Isa. 49:9).

Toys and trinkets are easily won, but the greatest things are greatly bought. The top-most place of power is always bought with blood. You may have the pinnacles if you have enough blood to pay. That is the conquest condition of the holy heights everywhere. The story of real heroisms is the story of sacrificial blood. The chiefest values in life and character are not blown across our way by vagrant winds. Great souls have great sorrows.

> Great truths are dearly bought, the common truths,
>   Such as men give and take from day to day,
> Come in the common walk of easy life,
>   Blown by the careless wind across our way.
>
> Great truths are greatly won, not found by chance
>   Nor wafted on the breath of summer dream;
> But grasped in the great struggle of the soul,
>   Hard buffeting with adverse wind and stream.
>
> But in the day of conflict, fear and grief,
>   When the strong hand of God, put forth in might,
> Plows up the subsoil of the stagnant heart,
>   And brings the imprisoned truth seed to the light.
>
> Wrung from the troubled spirit, in hard hours
>   Of weakness, solitude, perchance of pain,
> Truth sprints like harvest from the well-plowed field,
>   And the soul feels it has not wept in vain.

The capacity for knowing God enlarges as we are brought by Him into circumstances which oblige us to exercise faith; so, when difficulties beset our path let us thank God that He is taking trouble with us, and lean hard upon Him.

No discipline seems pleasant at the time, but painful. Later on, however, it produces a harvest of righteousness and peace for those who have been trained by it (Heb. 12:11).

There is a legend that tells of a German baron who, at his castle on the Rhine, stretched wires from tower to tower, that the winds might convert them into an aeolian harp. And the soft breezes played about the castle, but no music was born.

But one night there arose a great tempest, and hill and castle were smitten by the fury of the mighty winds. The baron went to the threshold to look out upon the terror of the storm, and the aeolian harp was filling the air with strains that rang out even above the clamor of the tempest. It needed the tempest to bring out the music!

And have we not known men whose lives have not given out any entrancing music in the day of a calm prosperity, but who, when the tempest drove against them have astonished their fellows by the power and strength of their music?

> Rain, rain
> Beating against the pane!
> How endlessly it pours
> Out of doors
> From the blackened sky—
> I wonder why!
>
> Flowers, flowers,
> Upspringing after showers,
> Blossoming fresh and fair,
> Everywhere!
> Ah, God has explained
> Why it rained!

You can always count on God to make the "later on" of discipline, if rightly overcome, a thousand times richer and fairer than if it had not happened. "No discipline seems pleasant at the time, but painful. Later on, however. . . ." What a yield!

"Should you then seek great things for yourself? Seek them not. For I will bring disaster on all people, declares the Lord, but wherever you go I will let you escape with your life" (Jer. 45:5).

We often pray to be delivered from calamities; we even trust that we shall be; but we do not pray to be made what we should be, in the very presence of the calamities; to live amid them, as long as they last, in the consciousness that we are held and sheltered by the Lord, and can therefore remain in the midst of them, so long as they continue, without any hurt. For forty days and nights, the Saviour was kept in the presence of Satan in the wilderness, and that, under circumstances of special trial, His human nature being weakened by want of food and rest. The furnace was heated seven times more than it was usually heated, but the three Hebrew children were kept amid its flames as calm and composed in the presence of the tyrant's last appliances of torture, as they were in his presence before their time of deliverance came. And all night Daniel sat among the lions, "and when Daniel was lifted from the den, no would was found on him, because he had trusted in his God" (Dan. 6:23).

DAY SEVENTEEN

Consider it pure joy, my brothers, whenever you face trials of many kinds, because you know that the testing of your faith develops perseverance. Perseverance must finish its work so that you may be mature and complete, not lacking anything (James 1:2–4).

There are saints today—always have been and always will be. But how is it that they are always with us? How does God make a saint? In this world we always have trials. It is this that makes the trail of a true leader. Paul, Luther, Savonarola, Knox, Wesley, Lincoln, Booth, Moody, Spurgeon, and many others have been put into storms in life. They are the noble leaders who bear evidence of having weathered the gales and wear the scars of conflict. They, like the great pine straining in the wind, exposed to the fury on a lone mountain crest, have come through triumphantly. Even though their torn and battered limbs have been almost ripped from them, their roots are deeply implanted in the Rock of Ages and could not be moved. They were bending in the tempest, but not breaking.

> A mountain tree, if it would see
> The fair horizons and the stars,
> Will never know a sheltered place
> Nor grow symmetrical in grace—
> Such trees must battle doggedly
> The blasts and bear the scars.
> —Selected

And will not God bring about justice for his chosen ones, who cry out to him day and night? . . . I tell you, he will see that they get justice, and quickly (Luke 18:7–8).

He gives strength to the weary and increases the power of the weak (Isa. 40:29).

How well does the Lord Jesus know our tendency to become weary and weak when the enemy presses us, when the darkness thickens around us, and when the stormy winds blow down around us, and especially when our prayers do not seem to prevail. In His great love He has given us purpose for just such troubling times as these. Instead of giving up we are to pray, and to keep on praying until He sends us the deliverance best for us. Unlike the unjust judge in Luke 8, who gave the widow justice only because she kept bothering him, God has promised us justice, "and quickly." Sad to say, only some know Him well enough to know that we do not trouble Him by our importunity, nor do we weary Him by our continual coming to Him. Someone once said, "Don't be afraid to go to God. He will never say, 'Come back when I'm not so busy.'"

DAY NINETEEN

"Love your neighbor as yourself" (Matt. 22:29).

Carry each other's burdens, and in this way you will fulfill the law of Christ (Gal. 6:2).

Angels are not fitted for sympathy, for they know nothing about human life. In a picture by Domenichino, there is an angel standing by the empty cross, touching with his finger one of the sharp points in the thorn-crown which the Saviour had worn. On his face there is the strangest bewilderment. He is trying to make out the mystery of sorrow. He knows nothing of suffering, for he has never suffered. There is nothing in the angel nature or in the angel life to interpret struggle or pain. The same is measurably true of untried human life. If we would be sons of consolation, our natures must be enriched by experience. We are not naturally gentle to all men. There is a harshness in us that needs to be mellowed. We are apt to be heedless of the feelings of others, to forget how many hearts are sore, and carry heavy burdens. We are not gentle toward sorrow, because our own hearts never have been plowed. The best universities cannot teach us the divine art of sympathy. We must walk in the deep valleys ourselves, and then we can be guides to other souls. We must feel the strain, and carry the burden, and endure the struggle ourselves, and then we can be touched, and can give help to others in life's sore stress and poignant need.

The righteous will flourish like a palm tree . . . (Ps. 92:12).

How meaningless this statement is by the psalmist, unless you are acquainted with palm trees. People who live in tropical and semi-tropical areas are so familiar with their graceful towering beauty, they are a very common tree to them. But I am sure that few realize what meanings the characteristics of this stately tree have. The first simile is life. The life of the tree comes through its center or heart. Just as all the other trees, it draws its moisture up through its roots from the earth. But instead of the sap going up on the outside between the bark and the wood of the tree, and so on up into the branches and twigs, as is true in most other trees, in the palm tree the sap goes up the very heart of the tree. Most trees can be killed by simply severing the bark completely around the tree about an inch or two. The life of the palm, however, does not lie so close under the surface and is not affected by surface injury. It must be completely cut off to be killed.

The same applies to "Palm-tree Christians." The Word of God states this so aptly in Romans 10:10, "For it is with your heart that you believe and are justified." A "Palm-tree Christian" is not affected by outward environment, but draws his life and strength through the heart.

The palm tree is perennially green. Life flows within its being continually. Those who are considered "Palm-tree Christians" never change. They are the same vibrant witnesses of God's grace day in and day out, because Jesus Christ Himself is "the same yesterday, today, and forever."

DAY TWENTY-ONE

I am still confident of this: I will see the goodness of the Lord in the land of the living (Ps. 27:13).

his encouraging testimony was written for us by the Psalmist, David, after he had gone through some shadowing experiences of severe trial and testing. More than once he was willing to give up in despair; to lie down and die. Not a few of his Psalms quake with his mournful dirges; and we come upon the man crying out in agony for a way to be rid of the violent storms of life. The sweet Psalmist of Israel reveals in Psalm 27 the secret of his confidence: "I will see the goodness of the Lord in the land of the living." That means in the present life, not in the life hereafter.

> Wrestling prayer can wonders do,
> Bring relief in deepest straits;
> Prayer can force a passage through
> Iron bars and brazen gates.

A supernatural deliverance was given to one who feared God. The heartening account is recorded in 2 Kings 4:4. A minister of God had died, leaving his widow and two sons in dire straits. They could not shoulder the responsibilities and soon the creditors came to take the widow's sons, her only means of support, to be slaves. In desperation the mother obeyed Elisha the prophet and thus received the blessing of God, who "sustains the fatherless and the widow." Pay a visit to this widow's cottage. It will stimulate your faith to learn what God did on her behalf.

When every prop is gone—all else but God—then He knows your heart cry is one of utter dependence upon Him. You can also experience the "hardest place in life" as being the sweetest. It is there one makes a fresh discovery of God.

*Surely goodness and love will follow me all the days of my life
(Ps. 23:6).*

Hudson Taylor once said: "The Lord *is* my Shepherd; *is*
on Sunday, *is* on Monday, and *is* through every day of
the week; *is* in January, *is* in December, and every
month of the year. *Is* at home, and *is* in China; *is* in peace,
and *is* in war; in abundance, and in penury!"

At another time he wrote: "All God's dealings are full of
blessing: He is good, and doeth good, good only, and continually. The believer who has taken the Lord as his
Shepherd can assuredly say in the words of the Psalmist:
'Surely goodness and love shall follow me all the days of my
life.' Hence we may be sure that the days of adversity, as
well as days of prosperity, are full of blessing. The believer
does not need to wait until he sees the reason of God's afflic-
tive dealings with him before he is satisfied; he knows that 'in
all things God works for the good of those who love him,
who have been called according to his purpose'" (Rom.
8:28).

The shepherd is responsible for the sheep; not the sheep
for the shepherd! The worst of it is that we sometimes think
we are both the shepherd and the sheep, and that we have
both to guide and follow! Happy are we when we realize that
He is responsible; that He goes before; and goodness and
mercy shall follow us!

This devotional thought may be read by someone who is
being severely tested almost to the breaking point! Someone
wondering about the tomorrows! He knows all about *your*
tomorrows, and is thinking in advance for *you!* Yes, *for
you!* For *you* He careth! Hide away in your heart the gracious promise: "How precious to me are your thoughts, O
God!"

DAY TWENTY-THREE

Then Solomon began to build the temple of the Lord. . . . He adorned the temple with precious stones (2 Chron. 3:1, 6).

Don't you know that you yourselves are God's temple? . . . (1 Cor. 3:16).

he stones from the wall said, "We come from the mountains far away, from the sides of the craggy hills. Fire and water have worked on us for ages, but made us only crags. Human hands have made us into a dwelling where the children of your immortal race are born, and suffer, and rejoice, and find rest and shelter, and learn the lessons set them by our Maker and yours. But we have passed through much to fit us for this. Gunpowder has rent our very heart; pickaxes have cleaved and broken us, it seemed to us often without design or meaning, as we lay misshapen stones in the quarry; but gradually we were cut into blocks, and some of us were chiseled with finer instruments to a sharper edge. But we are complete now, and are in our places, and are of service.

"You are in the quarry still, and not complete, and therefore to you, as once to us, much is inexplicable. But you are destined for a higher building, and one day you will be placed in it by hands not human, a living stone in a heavenly temple."

> In the still air the music lies unheard;
>   In the rough marble beauty hides unseen;
> To make the music and the beauty needs
>   The master's touch, the sculptor's chisel keen.
>
> Great Master, touch us with Thy skillful hands;
>   Let not the music that is in us die!
> Great Sculptor, hew and polish us; nor let,
>   Hidden and lost, thy form within us lie!

So Jacob was left alone, and a man wrestled with him till daybreak (Gen. 32:24).

God is wrestling with Jacob more than Jacob is wrestling with God. It was the Son of man, the Angel of the Covenant. It was God in human form pressing down and pressing out the old Jacob life; and ere the morning broke, God had prevailed and Jacob fell with his thigh dislocated. But as he fell, he fell into the arms of God, and there he clung and wrestled until the blessing came; and the new life was born and he arose from the earthly to the heavenly, the natural to the supernatural. And as he went forth that morning he was a weak and broken man, but God was there instead. "Then the man said, 'Your name will no longer be Jacob, but Israel, because you have struggled with God and with men and have overcome'" (Gen. 32:28).

Beloved, this must be a typical scene in every transformed life. There comes a crisis-hour to each of us, if God has called us to the highest and best, when all resources fail; when we face either ruin or something higher than we ever dreamed; when we must have help from God and yet, ere we can have it, we must let something go; we must cease from our own wisdom, strength, and righteousness, and become crucified with Christ and alive in Him. God knows how to lead us up to this crisis, and He knows how to lead us through.

Is He leading you thus? Is this the meaning of your deep trial, or your difficult surroundings, or that trying place through which you cannot go without Him, and yet you have not enough of Him to give you the victory?

Oh, turn to Jacob's God! Cast yourself helplessly at His feet. Die to your strength and wisdom in His loving arms and rise, like Jacob, into His strength and all-sufficiency. There is no way out of your hard and narrow place but at the top. You must get deliverance by rising higher and coming into a new experience with God. Oh, may it bring you into all that is meant by the revelation of the Mighty One of Jacob!

"My Father, if it is possible, may this cup be taken from me. Yet not as I will, but as you will" (Matt. 26:39).

". . . Shall I not drink the cup the Father has given me?" (John 18:11).

o have a sympathizing God we must have a suffering Saviour, and there is no true fellow-feeling with another save in the heart of him who has been afflicted like him.

We cannot do good to others save at a cost to ourselves, and our afflictions are the price we pay for our ability to sympathize. He who would be a helper, must first be a sufferer. He who would be a saviour must somewhere and somehow have been upon a cross; and we cannot have the highest happiness of life in helping others without tasting the cup which Jesus drank. Though Christ prayed to be spared from the suffering of the Cross, when He realized His suffering was imperative to God's plan of redemption, He submitted willingly. So too we, when called on to suffer for another's good, must suffer willingly.

The most comforting of David's psalms were pressed out by suffering; and if Paul had not had his thorn in the flesh we had missed much of that tenderness which quivers in so many of his letters.

The present circumstance, which presses so hard against you (if surrendered to Christ), is the best shaped tool in the Father's hand to chisel you for eternity. Trust Him, then. Do not push away the instrument lest you lose its work.

> Strange and difficult indeed
>   We may find it,
> But the blessing that we need
>   Is behind it.

The school of suffering graduates rare scholars.

Then Peter got down out of the boat and walked on the water to Jesus. But when he saw the wind, he was afraid and, beginning to sink, cried out, "Lord, save me!" (Matt. 14:29–30).

Peter had a little faith in the midst of his doubts, says Bunyan; and so with crying and coming he was brought to Christ.

But here you see that sight was a hindrance; the waves were none of his business when once he had set out; all Peter had any concern with was the pathway of light that came gleaming across the darkness from where Christ stood. If it was tenfold Egypt beyond that, Peter had to call to look and see.

When the Lord shall call to you over the waters, "Come," step gladly forth. Look not for a moment away from Him.

Not by measuring the waves can you prevail; not by gauging the wind will you grow strong; to scan the danger may be to fall before it; to pause at the difficulties is to have them break above your head. Lift up your eyes unto the hills, and go forward—there is no other way.

> Dost thou fear to launch away?
>   Faith lets go to swim!
> Never will He let thee go;
> 'Tis by trusting thou shalt know
>   Fellowship with Him.

The Lord, the King of Israel, is with you; never again will you fear any harm. . . . He will delight in you, he will quiet you with his love, he will rejoice over you with singing (Zeph. 3:15, 17).

Quietness amid the dash of the storm. We sail the lake with Him still; and as we reach its middle waters, far from land, under midnight skies, suddenly a great storm sweeps down. Earth and hell seem arrayed against us, and each billow threatens to overwhelm. Then He arises from His sleep, and rebukes the winds and the waves; His hand waves benediction and repose over the rage of the tempestuous elements. His voice is heard above the scream of the wind in the cordage and the conflict of the billows. Can you not hear it? And there is instantly a great calm. "He will quiet you with his love." *Quietness amid the loss of inward consolations.* He sometimes withdraws these, because we make too much of them. We are tempted to look at our joy, our ecstasies, our transports, or our visions, with too great complacency. Then love for love's sake, withdraws them. But, by His grace, He leads us to distinguish between them and Himself. He draws nigh, and whispers the assurance of His presence. Thus an infinite calm comes to keep our heart and mind. "He will quiet you with his love."

Awake, north wind, and come, south wind! Blow on my garden, that its fragrance may spread abroad (Song of Songs 4:16).

The meaning of this prayer is found in the fact that, as delicious odors may lie *latent* in a spice tree, so *graces* may lie unexercised and undeveloped in a Christian's heart. There is many a plant of profession; but from the ground there breathes forth no fragrance of holy affections or of godly deeds. The same winds blow on the thistle bush and on the spice tree, but only *one* of them gives out rich odors.

Sometimes God sends severe blasts of trial upon His children to develop their graces. Just as torches burn most brightly when swung to and fro; just as the juniper plant smells sweetest when flung into the flames; so the richest qualities of a Christian often come out under the north wind of suffering and adversity. Bruised hearts often emit the fragrance that God loveth to smell.

> I had a tiny box, a precious box
> Of human love—my spikenard of great price;
> I kept it close within my heart of hearts,
> And scarce would lift the lid lest it should waste
> Its perfume on the air. One day a strange
> Deep sorrow came with crushing weight, and fell
> Upon my costly treasure, sweet and rare,
> And broke the box to atoms. All my heart
> Rose in dismay and sorrow at this waste,
> But as I mourned, behold a miracle
> Of grace Divine. My human love was changed
> To Heaven's own, and poured in healing streams
> On other broken hearts, while soft and clear
> A voice above me whispered, "Child of Mine,
> With comfort wherewith thou art comforted,
> From this time forth, go comfort others,
> And thou shalt know blest fellowship with Me,
> Whose broken heart of love hath healed the world."

DAY TWENTY-NINE

Grain must be ground to make bread (Isa. 28:28).

Poverty, hardship and misfortune have pressed many a life to moral heroism and spiritual greatness. Difficulty challenges energy and perseverance. It calls into activity the strongest qualities of the soul. It was the weights on father's old clock that kept it going. Many a head wind has been utilized to make port. God has appointed opposition as an incentive to faith and holy activity.

The most illustrious characters of the Bible were bruised and threshed and ground into bread for the hungry. Abraham's diploma styles him as "the father of the faithful." That was because he stood at the head of his class in affliction and obedience.

Jacob suffered severe threshings and grindings. Joseph was bruised and beaten and had to go through Potiphar's kitchen and Egypt's prison to get to his throne.

David, hunted like a partridge on the mountain, bruised, weary and footsore, was ground into bread for a kingdom. Paul never could have been bread for Caesar's household if he had not endured the bruising, whippings and stonings. He was ground into fine flour for the royal family.

Like combat, like victory. If for you He has appointed special trials, be assured that in His heart He has kept for you a special place. A soul sorely bruised is a soul elect.

. . . And your strength will equal your days (Deut. 33:25).

I t is not the great achievement of the Red Sea crossing by Moses and the Israelites that is so stupendous and miraculous. The awesomeness of the Wilderness Journey is the fact that approximately three million people were sustained for forty years in a small, dry, fruitless desert. Have you thought of what it must have been like to merely exist from *day to day* with every human means for survival out of reach? Let us look at a few facts to see how impossible it would have been for Moses and his people to rely upon their own means of subsistence: To get through the Red Sea in one night they had to have a space at least three miles wide, so they could walk 5,000 abreast. If they walked doublefile, it would have been 800 miles long, and it would have taken them 35 days and nights to get through. At the end of each day of the journey they would have needed space two-thirds the size of the state of Rhode Island for them to camp. This would have been a total of 750 square miles. The amount of food for consumption alone is absolutely astounding when you consider the fact that they were traveling in a country where there was no abundance of natural food to be found. Just the amount needed to keep from starving would have added up to 1,500 tons a day. But to feed them the way we would eat, it would take at least 4,000 tons. Just to haul it would take two freight trains, each one a mile long. At to-day's prices it would cost $4 million a day! Then consider the amount of water required for barest necessities of drinking and washing dishes each day. It has been calculated that they would have to have 11 million gallons every single day. Think of the gigantic task of hauling water. It would have taken a freight train with tank cars, 1,800 miles long!

Now Moses may or may not have had to do the figuring for managing the survival of his people, but God surely knew the cost! It may be more easily understood why Moses hesitated to be the great emancipator of God's enslaved people if he had had any inkling as to what an immense chore there was before him. We do know for a surety that he knew the land, its seasons and size. But God was the Provider, not Moses. The requirement for him and the multitude was to proceed day by day. God supplied for just one day at a time. To think that they did not even have to transport their food and water. God took care of them—and for 14,600 days!

Part 3

Fall

See how he scatters
   his lightning about him,
  bathing the depths
   of the sea.
This is the way
   he governs the nations
  and provides food
   in abundance.

Job 36:30–31

. . . we all shrivel up like a leaf . . . (Isa. 64:6).

How does the leaf in autumn fade? It is true that certain trees renew in their autumn foliage the same color that marked them in their budding time of spring, but with fuller, brighter hues. Nature does not die drably! She puts on her most gorgeous robes in autumn and dies gloriously. She goes down with her gay banners waving, smiles back to us as she leaves us. God speaks to His own comforting messages at all seasons and at all times.

Why should we have a dread of the transition? God has made the "valley of the shadow" as beautiful as the day-break. In Charles Kingsley's last hour he was heard to whisper, "How beautiful is God."

> If peace be in the heart
> The wildest winter storm is filled with beauty
> The very trees and stones, all catch a ray of glory
> If peace be in the heart.

He gave us the secret of victory. It is the peace of God, passing all understanding that makes all the way long a good journey. "My peace I give to you."

> The air is full of hints of grief,
> Strange voices touched with pain,
> The pathos of the falling leaf,
> The rustling of the rain.
> —Anonymous

DAY TWO

While Jesus was in Bethany . . . a woman came to him with an alabaster jar of very expensive perfume, which she poured on his head. . . . When the disciples saw this, they were indignant. "Why this waste?" they asked (Matt. 26:6–8).

I s it true that the woman's perfume was wasted when she poured it upon her Christ? Suppose she did not break the alabaster box nor pour out the perfume? Could there have been a remembrance of her act of love? It surely would not have been recorded within the gospel story. Surely her deed would not have been told over the whole world. She broke the vase and poured it out. She lost it, all of it. It was her sacrifice. Now the fragrance from the precious perfume fills all the earth.

"Our lives must be kept, carefully preserved from waste," say those who are not close enough to their Lord to stoop down and anoint His feet. Little they know that the reward will be not theirs to claim. They will not have honor to cherish. Only if life is poured out in loving service will it be a blessing to the world. Then and only then will there be reward. God will remember such a giver forever.

". . . whoever loses his life for me will find it" (Matt. 16:25).

In the Talmud there is a story of a peasant worker who fell in love with the daughter of his wealthy employer. She returned his love and, despite her father's violent objections, married him. Aware of her husband's ardent love for learning, she insisted that he go to the great rabbinical academy at Jerusalem to slake his intellectual thirst. He studied for twelve years while she, disowned by her family, suffered in poverty and loneliness. Though still eager for advanced studies, he returned home. When he reached the door of his house, he overheard his wife saying to a neighbor that even though the pain of separation seemed more than she could bear, she hoped and prayed that he would return to the academy for further study.

Without a word to anyone, he went back to the school for twelve years more of study. Once again he turned determined footsteps toward his native village, but this time all Palestine was singing his praises as the most brilliant and scholarly mind of his generation. As he entered the market place, he was caught in the crowd of a reception committee that had gathered to honor their native son. While people were pressing about him, he saw a woman—her body bent, her face wrinkled—desperately trying to break through to reach him. Suddenly he realized that this prematurely old woman, whom the milling crowd ignored and pushed back, was his beloved wife.

"Let her through," he shouted. "Let her through. It is she, not I, whom you should honor—she who sacrificed while I studied. Had it not been for her willingness to work and wait, to serve and suffer, I would be today a peasant laborer and not Rabbi Akeba."

Today we find ourselves conditioned only for the spectacular. We scan our newspaper only for momentous news—our admiration is so linked with the glamorous that we have almost forgotten the usual everyday activities of the average person. We have been so busy acclaiming and applauding the amazing exploits of our military technicians, the extraordinary maneuvers of national and world statesmen as they direct the destinies of great masses of people, and the miraculous discoveries and contributions of scientific geniuses and industrial giants that we have failed to appreciate those individuals and accomplishments which have played and presented their vital roles in the drama of life—toiling quietly but effectively behind the scenes, performing only so-called minor parts.

> Sometimes we find within the heart
>   Of those whom other folks pass by
> A strong desire to do their part,
>   To bless the world before they die.

Jesus answered, "Everyone who drinks this water will be thirsty again, but whoever drinks the water I give him will never thirst. Indeed, the water I give him will become in him a spring of water welling up to eternal life" (John 4:13–14).

To the heart that is hungering and thirsting after God and His fullness—for a drink from the living springs, this promise will be found literally true. Come thirsty one, bring your cup of need to God's measureless supply. Come and drink. Yes, drink abundantly.

Though millions their thirst now are slaking,
  It never runs dry:
And millions may still come partaking,
  It never runs dry.

An eastern caravan was overtaken once in the desert with a failure of the water supply. The accustomed fountains were all dried; the oasis was a desert. They stopped an hour before sunset to find, after a day of scorching heat, that they were perishing for want of water. Vainly they explored the usual wells, but they were all dry. Dismay was upon all faces; despair was in all hearts. Suddenly an old man approached the sheik and advised him to unloose the two beautiful deer that he was taking home as a present to his bride. Surely the sensitive nostrils of the deer would detect the presence of water if any was to be found. Their tongues were protruding with thirst; their bosoms heaved with distress, but as they were led out to the borders of the camp, they lifted up their heads and sniffed the air. Then, with unerring instinct, with a course as straight as an arrow and speed as swift as the wind, they darted off across the desert. Swift horsemen followed close behind, and an hour or two later hastened back with the good news that water had been found. The camp moved with shouts of rejoicing to the newly discovered fountains.

DAY FIVE

. . . I know whom I have believed, and am convinced that he is able to guard what I have entrusted to him for that day (2 Tim. 1:12).

A most unusual incident occurred in colorful Mexico City a few years ago. A famous artist had painted a beautiful picture, and it was being displayed upon the walls of a new, ultramodern hotel. The scene was one of the charming beauty spots of the country landscape. It depicted with lucid clarity the rolling country landscape, quiet fields, purling streams and a touch of virgin forest, carpeted with gorgeous flowers.

Across the top of the canvas four words were painted which stood out in bold outline: "God Does Not Exist." A strange bit of lettering to be found on such a famous work of art!

Spellbound visitors surged past the painting every day.

One evening a large group of young men entered the room that housed the painting. They quietly and calmly removed paint cans and brushes from kits strapped to their shoulders and were soon busily at work. Suddenly they stepped back and the throng pressing against the doorway caught a glimpse of the masterpiece. At first they could see no change, but continued scrutiny revealed that three words in the caption had been brushed completely from the canvas. One word remained—"God." Under the soft lights which were thrown upon the picture, that one glorious word was emblazoned—it shone like a brilliant in a monarch's crown.

More than anything else that may be needed—more than changed conditions, more than release from pressure—is a vigorous faith in God, a rediscovery of Him who knows the paths of a hundred million stars and knows the way through every valley of difficulty and over every mountain of trial. Renew confidence in God; rediscover God, the mighty God—a match for mighty needs!

The apostles said to the Lord, "Increase our faith!" (Luke 17:5).

A crowd of five thousand men, besides an uncounted number of women and children, were gathered on a hillside in Galilee overlooking the little lake. In this great host of people who had come to listen to the Master was one small boy who wanted to be of help. Just one boy would not seem to matter much. Yet because of his faith and obedience people all over the world for two thousand years have marveled at the incident in which he played a major role.

The sun was just setting. The people had been listening all day to Jesus as He mingled with them. It was no wonder that the children were restless and hungry. They had had no food for the entire day. The disciples concerned themselves with preparations for a meal. Jesus had mentioned that the crowd must have something to eat before starting homeward. Feed them—with what? There was no place nearby where they could get food.

Hoping some would share if they had brought lunches with them, the disciples moved through the throng asking for food. A small lad tugged on Andrew's arm. "Here is my basket. There are but five loaves and two fishes." Utterly amazed Andrew took the basket to Jesus. Andrew had begun to despair for carrying out such an obviously empty gesture in obedience to the commands of his Master. In the hands of the Master, the small basket of lunch became enough to feed the whole multitude. After all had eaten, there were still twelve baskets full of the left-overs!

Who are we to judge what God can, or cannot do? He made the world! He made all that is in it! He made the laws of nature! He rules the whole of creation as He wills! *We are the created, not the creators!*

Emerson so fittingly penned these words: "All I have seen teaches me to trust the Creator for all I have not seen."

DAY SEVEN

We are hard pressed on every side, but not crushed; perplexed, but not in despair; persecuted, but not abandoned; struck down, but not destroyed (2 Cor. 4:8–9).

George Matheson, the great Scottish preacher, who when he was told by a famous oculist that he was going blind, wrote these lovely words: "O love that will not let me go!—I rest my weary soul on thee." Also, "O joy that seekest me through pain, I cannot close my heart to Thee: I trace the rainbow through the rain;"—listen to these lines from his pen:

"There are times when things look very dark to me—so dark that I have to wait even for *hope*. A long-deferred fulfillment carries its own pain, but to wait for hope, to see no glimmer of a prospect and yet refuse to despair; to have nothing but night before the casement and yet to keep the casement open for possible stars; to have a vacant place in my heart and yet to allow that place to be filled by no inferior presence—that is the grandest patience in the universe. It is Job in the tempest; it is Abraham on the road to Moriah; it is Moses in the desert of Midian; it is the Son of man in the Garden of Gethsemane."

It takes a real faith to trace the rainbow through the rain, but it takes the storm-cloud to make the rainbow, and George Matheson learned to have a child-like trust, and his testimony has blessed millions throughout this generation.

> What then? Shall we sit idly down and say
> The night hath come; it is no longer day?
> Yet as the evening twilight fades away
> The sky is filled with stars, invisible to day.

"Why are you downcast, O my soul? Why so disturbed within me? Put your hope in God, for I will yet praise him, my Savior and my God" (Ps. 42:11).

"Everything is possible for him who believes" (Mark 9:23).

hat should be the attitude of a Christian when placed in a difficult and trying situation—a place of severe testing? There can be but one attitude! A simple and unwavering trust in God! A refusal to look *at* the difficult circumstance, but *above* it. The only sure way to do this is to live very close to God. As the turbo-supercharger enables an airplane to maintain full power at an altitude of thirty thousand feet, where an ordinary plane has lost four-fifths of its power, so the Christian who walks with his God, listening and obeying, keeps strong at the toughest heights of life. The fact is that God is stronger than any temptation and danger; and the person who has God in his heart is unconquerable.

It is true that God often seems to place His children in positions of profound difficulty, leading them into a tight corner—from which there is no way of escape—contriving a situation which no human judgment would have permitted.

During such periods, the words of Jesus quoted above take on added significance. It should be clearly understood that this kind of faith in God is the most practical approach to the problems and testings of life—it is not sense, or sight, or reason, but taking God at His word. Experience reveals that such a faith will not make the sun rise sooner, but it will make the night seem shorter.

DAY NINE

These have come so that your faith—of greater worth than gold . . .
may be proved genuine and may result in praise, glory and honor
when Jesus Christ is revealed (1 Peter 1:7).

A story is told by Francis Browne of a little pilgrim band sitting by the seashore recounting their losses. One tells of a ship that went down with all his household, and another, the sweet memories of a lost youth, and others of vanished gold, of proud honors gone, and of faithless friends. A stranger, seemingly free from all sorrow, said:

> Sad losses have ye met,
> But mine is heavier yet:
> For a believing heart hath gone from me.

"Alas!" said the pilgrims, "Thine, stranger, is life's last and heaviest loss."

Life's greatest loss is the loss of faith. "Christ's anxiety to retain Peter's faith," says one writer, "can only be explained one way. He did not interfere between him and failure, but He did interfere between him and the loss of faith. A man is lost when honor, truth, and character are gone; but when faith has gone, he has suffered the greatest loss."

*Who among you fears the Lord and obeys the word of his servant?
Let him who walks in the dark, who has no light, trust in the name of
the Lord and rely on his God (Isa. 50:10).*

The following words were brushed on a lovely hand-painted scroll: "Trust in the dark brings triumph at the dawn!" These words bring to mind the years of testing for Moses—his dark years—out in the waste places of the arid Sinai Desert. It was *faith in the dark*. Luxurious surroundings had been Moses' environment for forty years. Now he was to spend that same length of time in absence from those comforts. Humanly speaking it would be almost impossible to bear the strain. He had a secret Resource. "He persevered because he saw Him who is invisible." *God* was by his side in the desolate waste, and Moses experienced His lovingkindness. Moses knew his God as "a Rock in a weary land," and when the enduring was near breaking, he found himself hidden beneath its Shadow. He drank from the desert streams and thirsted not.

The day of the great revelation finally came to Moses. It was at the burning bush he learned of his great commission. He accepted, though reluctantly. He still was obedient at any cost. As time passed we see him as a God-trained leader standing on the shores of a seemingly impossible situation with his trusting throng. With no visible way before them God commands them to go forward. "By faith" Moses obeys. "By faith" Moses takes his flock through the Red Sea. His obedience gave birth to the faith that caused the Almighty Arm to stretch forth across the sea and make dry land. What an Omnipotent God! What a joyous experience! Oh, believer, give God the chance to perform an answer to your prayer of faith!

DAY ELEVEN

This is the victory that has overcome the world, even our faith (1 John 5:4).

During a hillside vesper service, the message brought by His messenger was on "The Signs of the Times and World Conditions." Many were assembled there, a large group of believers, facing the future—so unseen; so unknown!—facing facts and grim realities. The question uppermost in all hearts was: "How are God's children to meet the testings that are certain to be theirs in the months ahead?" Believers cannot be ostriches, burying their heads in the sand in a refusal to see things as they are. They must be prepared to face the issues! But how is this to be done? God prepares His own for the awful days and makes them *overcomers!*

> He said not,
>   "Thou shalt not be Tempested;
>   Thou shalt not be Travailed;
>   Thou shalt not be Afflicted;"
> But He said,
>   "Thou shalt not be Overcome!"

". . . behold, he goeth before you into Galilee" (Matt. 28:7 KJV).

hen a Christian loses heart, he loses everything! To keep one's heart in the midst of life's stream and to maintain a front that knows no defeat in the face of its difficulties, is not an achievement that springs from anything that a laboratory can demonstrate, or that logic can affirm. It is an achievement of faith! If you lose your sky, you will soon lose your earth.

We quote a few helpful excerpts from a message given by a minister in Scotland: "Nothing is more beautiful than our Lord's forethought! He was always thinking ahead of the disciples. When He sent them to prepare the Passover there was found an upper room furnished and prepared. His plans were not only for *that* day. He was always in advance of time! When the disciples came back from fishing, Jesus was on the seashore with a fire of coals and fish laid thereon. In the morning He thinks of the day before you are astir! He is waiting long before you are awake. His anticipations are along all the way of life before you!

"After the resurrection, the disciples were bewildered and the way looked black! But the angel said, 'Behold, He goeth before you into Galilee;' He is always thinking ahead! preparing ahead."

You will discover His insight! His oversight! and His foresight! You may not always see Him, but you can walk by faith in the dark if you know that He sees you; and can sing as you journey, even through the night.

DAY THIRTEEN

Let us fix our eyes on Jesus, the author and perfecter of our faith, who for the joy set before him endured the cross, scorning its shame, and sat down at the right hand of the throne of God (Heb. 12:2).

If we will but catch a glimpse of the glory awaiting us in yonder city, new strength will be given us. Our Forerunner "endured the cross, scorning its shame."

The fight in this eleventh hour is not with flesh and blood—it is a fight of faith. With an anointed vision we discern the trend of the time in which we live and our call is renewed to "contend for the faith that was once for all entrusted to the saints." Are we guarding that faith as a sacred treasure? "When the Son of Man comes, will he find faith on the earth?" (Luke 18:8). Searching question! Can we sing from the depths of our hearts:

> Faith of our fathers! living still,
> In spite of dungeon, fire, and sword;
> O how our hearts beat high with joy
> Whene'er we hear that glorious word.
>
> Our fathers chained in prisons dark,
> Were still in heart and conscience free;
> How sweet would be their children's fate,
> If they, like them, should die for Thee!
>
> Faith of our fathers! we will strive
> To win all nations unto Thee;
> And through the truth that comes from God,
> Mankind shall then indeed be free.
>
> Faith of our fathers, holy faith
> We will be true to Thee till death.
> —Frederick W. Faber

But if we hope for what we do not yet have, we wait for it patiently (Rom. 8:25).

It is a wonderful thing to be "alive unto God," and I believe it is the only way to be kept alive to every good thing that is worth anything. We can so live in God that we are in touch with the past, the present, the future. The most interesting things are those we haven't seen. The most of life is before us, because life is not extension, it is satisfaction. We have never seen His face yet; we have never seen our dear ones in their new bodies; and we are yet to see the coming of Christ; we are to see Him take to Himself His great power, and reign from the rivers to the ends of the earth. All this is before us.

"The grass withers and the flowers fall, but the word of our God stands forever" (Isa. 40:8).

The Bible is a great treasury of reserved blessing. There has not been a chapter, a line, a word, added to it since the pen of inspiration wrote the final Amen; yet every new generation finds new things in this Holy Book. How true it is in every individual experience. As younger people we study the Bible, but many of the precious verses have little or no meaning for us. The light, the comfort, the help are all there, but we do not see it. We cannot see it until we have a fuller sense of need. The rich truths seem to be hiding away, refusing to disclose their meaning. When we begin to experience the struggles, trials, and conflicts of real life, then the new senses begin to reveal themselves in the old familiar sentences. Promises that seemed as if they were written in invisible ink now begin to glow with rich meaning, flash out like newly lighted lamps, and pour bright beams upon the path of life. The light is not new. It had shone there all the while, but could not be seen until now because other lights were shining about obscuring this one.

Daniel Webster once said that he "believed that the Bible is to be believed and understood in the plain and obvious meaning of its passages; for I can not persuade myself that a book intended for the instruction and conversion of the whole world should cover its true meaning in any such mystery and doubt that none but critics and philosophers can discover it."

"For God so loved the world that he gave his one and only Son, that whoever believes in him shall not perish but have eternal life" (John 3:16).

We share a gem from the heart of Dr. Hinson. While speaking from the pulpit about a year after the commencement of the disease from which he ultimately died, Dr. Hinson said, "I remember a year ago when a man in this city said, 'You are a dying man.' I walked the five miles from his office out to my home—and I looked across toward that majestic mountain that I love and I looked at the river in which I rejoice, and I looked at the stately trees that are always God's own poetry to my soul. Then in the evening, I looked up into the great sky when God was lighting His lamps, and I said, 'I may not see you many more times, but mountain, I shall be alive when you are gone; and river, I shall be alive when you cease running toward the sea; and stars, I shall be alive when you have fallen from your sockets in the great down pulling of the universe.'"

*. . . my foes will rejoice when I fall. But I trust in your unfailing love;
my heart rejoices in your salvation (Ps. 13:4–5).*

Faith is not clinging—it is letting go."

Somewhere we have read a story that goes like this:

"A traveller upon a lonely road was set upon by bandits who robbed him of all he had. They then led him into the depths of the forest. There in the darkness they tied a rope to the limb of a great tree, and bade him catch hold of the end of it. Swinging him out into the blackness of surrounding space, they told him he was hanging over the brink of a giddy precipice. The moment he let go he would be dashed to pieces on the rocks below. And then they left him. His soul was filled with horror at the awful doom impending. He clutched despairingly the end of the swaying rope. But each dreadful moment only made his fate more sure. His strength steadily failed. At last he could hold on no longer. The end had come. His clenched fingers relaxed their convulsive grip. He fell—six inches, to the solid earth at his feet! It was only a ruse of the robbers to gain time in escaping. And when he let go it was not to death, but to the safety which had been waiting him through all his time of terror."

Clutching will not save anyone from hopelessness. It is only Satan's trick to keep you from being afforded security and peace in the solid promises of God. And all the while you are swinging over the supposed precipice of fear and mistrust. Let go! It is God's plan that you fall—not to defeat, but into His arms, the solid Rock. As soon as you recognize your sheer helplessness and your failing strength, you let go; and falling upon Him, your fear goes, your mistrust goes, and the blessed assurance comes forever. For *He* —not your clinging but— "*He* will save *his* people from their sins."

They . . . came to the iron gate leading to the city. It opened for them by itself, and they went through it (Acts 12:10).

The chains that bound Peter when he was in prison were struck off. He followed the angel sent to help him. On the way out of prison they came to an impossible barrier, the iron gate leading into the city. But it "opened for them by itself." "If you will do all the possible things, God will take care of the impossible." God did nothing for Peter that night that Peter could do for himself. If the iron gate is locked and barred and staring you in the face, God's call is to do for yourself whatever He has asked you to do, and trust Him to do the rest.

The Lord, in that great Sermon on the Mount, said, "Therefore do not worry about tomorrow, for tomorrow will worry about itself. Each day has enough trouble of its own" (Matt. 7:34).

While we let ourselves worry, we are not trusting. But still it is a habit of ours to worry. Bishop Quayle had a sense of humor concerning himself. So he tells humorously of a time when he sat in his study worrying over many things. He relates that finally the Lord came to him and said, "Quayle, you go to bed; I'll sit up the rest of the night."

DAY NINETEEN

In my distress I called to the Lord; I cried to my God for help. . . . He reached down from on high and took hold of me; he drew me out of deep waters (Ps. 18:6, 16).

God does not grant the necessary grace before the trial. He builds the bridge when we reach the river. We often fear that we shall sink under the fiery trials that we see others endure. We see in the distance and are afraid of the mystery and anguish of what is to befall us; but we have not yet reached the crises, and grace is not vouchsafed before it is needed. "Jesus comes with our distress."

"Give thanks to the Lord, for his love endures forever" (2 Chron. 20:21).

artin Luther once wrote these words, "When I cannot pray, I always sing."

In Chronicles there is a thrilling narrative about a battle won through praise. Jehoshaphat was told that a great multitude was coming against him from across the sea. He fully realized the difficulty of the situation and went to the Lord with his trouble. His was a humble prayer: "We have no power to face this vast army that is attacking us. We do not know what to do, but our eyes are upon you" (2 Chron. 20:12). Not upon the greatness of the difficulty, but upon Him.

Then Jehoshaphat appointed singers to go forth before the army singing, "Give thanks to the Lord, for his love endures forever" (20:21). They did this even though there was not one visible sign of the promised salvation of the Lord. Right in the very face of battle they sang, "Give thanks to the Lord." The inspired record says, "As they began to sing and praise, the Lord set ambushes against the men of Ammon and Moab and Mount Seir who were invading Judah, and they were defeated" (20:22). Two of the allied opposing armies began to fight the third, and when they had demolished them, they turned upon each other until the valley was filled with dead bodies—no one had escaped. Jehoshaphat's army had more than victory, for we read, "there was so much plunder that it took three days to collect it" (20:25). They were much richer at the end of the trial than at the beginning.

There are two songs in Jehoshaphat's great battle: the song of praise before and the song of deliverance afterward. We also should have two songs: a song in the Valley of Beracah (blessing), praising God for the fulfillment of all that He has promised; but it is more precious to have the song of praise before the victory—praising Him without sight or feeling while we see Him set ambushes against the enemy and complete the victory.

DAY TWENTY-ONE

I sought the Lord, and he answered me; he delivered me from all my fears (Ps. 34:4).

I once heard the famous Scottish preacher, John McNeil, relate this personal incident. During his boyhood in Scotland, he worked a long distance from home. The walk home took him through a dense forest and across a wide ravine. The ravine was known to house such nefarious tenants as wild animals and robber gangs. Darkness would often gather before he got to the woods, and he said, "How I dreaded to make the last part of the trip! I never went through those woods without trembling with fear.

"One night it was especially dark, but I was aware that something or someone was moving stealthily toward me. I was sure it was a robber. A voice called out, and its eerie tone struck my heart cold with fear. I thought I was finished. Then came a second call, and this time I could hear the voice saying, 'John, is that you?' It was my father's voice. He had known my fear of the ravine and the darkness of the forest, and he had come out to meet me. My father took hold of my hand and put his arm around me; I never had a sweeter walk in my life. His coming changed the whole trip."

That is God's relationship to you and me! He is your Father and my Father. Through the darkness and mist we hear His voice—He has come to meet us. Just at the time we need Him, He will be there. Through the darkest moment of life our heavenly Father says, "FEAR NOT! Here is My hand! I will walk the rest of the way with you."

Give thanks to the Lord, for he is good; his love endures forever (1 Chron. 16:34).

Praise the Lord, O my soul; and forget not all his benefits (Ps. 103:2).

Harvest is ended. There is a song in the air—a song of joy-filled hearts and thanksgiving. Goodness and mercy have followed throughout every day of the year. We have been loaded, yea, overloaded with His benefits and manifold tokens of His love and mercy. "He cares for us." Our testings and trials have been buried beneath His mercies which outnumber the waves of the sea. We praise God that He saw us through the tempests we thought would pull us under. He is our own God; we are the flock of His pasture and the people of His hand.

"May the peoples praise you, O God; may all the peoples praise you. Then the land will yield its harvest, and God, our God, will bless us. God will bless us, and all the ends of the earth will fear him" (Ps. 67:5–7).

Fall is the season in which we celebrate Thanksgiving Day, a sacred day for retrospection—a day also for spiritual inventory—a day for family reunions, fellowship with old friends and neighbors, sharing our bounties with those less favored. If throughout the past year earthborn clouds have blotted out the sunshine of your spiritual sky, may there be a rift in the clouds today so that you can see through to the land of pure delight where saints immortal reign.

". . . He who sacrifices thank offerings honors me, and he prepares the way so that I may show him the salvation of God" (Ps. 50:23).

We read in the Book of Joshua how the walls of Jericho fell flat after they were compassed about seven days. God had declared that He had given them the city. Faith reckoned this to be true, so they began their march around the walls using as their only weapon that which indicated triumph—a ram's horn! Unbelief might have prayed this kind of prayer, "O Lord, make the walls totter just a little, or loosen a few stones so that we may have a sign that Thou art going to answer our prayer, and then we will praise Thee." Prudence might have said, "It is not safe to shout until the victory is actually won, lest the Lord be dishonored before the people and be greatly humiliated." This would not have been faith at all. They acted on the authority of God's Word and shouted the shout of faith before there was a sign of encouragement, and the Lord accomplished the rest. It is after we make a full commitment that "he will bring it to pass."

How many walls of difficulty would fall flat were we to simply march around them with shouts of praise? As we compass walls with praise, the Lord has promised to "compass us about with songs of deliverance."

There is a legend which tells of two angels who come from heaven every morning and go on their rounds all the day long. One is the Angel of Requests. The other is the Angel of Thanksgiving. Each carries a basket. The one belonging to the Angel of Requests is soon filled to overflowing, for everyone pours into it great handfuls of requests; but when the day is ended, the Angel of Thanksgiving has in his basket only two or three small contributions of gratitude.

"Everything is possible for him who believes" (Mark 9:23).

T he "all things" do not always come simply for the asking, for the reason that God is ever seeking to teach us the way of faith, and in our training in the faith life there must be room for the trial of faith, the discipline of faith, the patience of faith, the courage of faith, and often many stages are passed before we really realize what is the end of faith, namely, the victory of faith.

Real moral fiber is developed through discipline of faith. You have made your request of God, but the answer does not come. What are you to do?

Keep on believing God's Word; never be moved away from it by what you see or feel, and thus as you stand steady, enlarged power and experience is being developed. The fact of looking at the apparent contradiction as to God's Word and being unmoved from your position of faith make you stronger on every other line.

Often God delays purposely, and the delay is just as much an answer to your prayer as is the fulfillment when it comes.

In the lives of all the great Bible characters, God worked thus. Abraham, Moses and Elijah were not great in the beginning, but were made great through the discipline of their faith, and only thus were they fitted for the positions to which God had called them.

For example, in the case of Joseph whom the Lord was training for the throne of Egypt, we read in the Psalms:

"The word of the Lord tried him." It was not the prison life with its hard beds or poor food that tried him, but it was the word God had spoken into his heart in the early years concerning elevation and honor which were greater than his brethren were to receive; it was this which was ever before him, when every step in his career made it seem more and more impossible of fulfillment, until he was there imprisoned, and all in innocency, while others who were perhaps justly

101

incarcerated, were released, and he was left to languish alone.

These were hours that tried his soul, but hours of spiritual growth and development, that, "when his word came" (the word of release), found him fitted for the delicate task of dealing with his wayward brethren, with a love and patience only surpassed by God Himself.

No amount of persecution tries like such experiences as these. When God has spoken of His purpose to do, and yet the days go on and He does not do it, that is truly hard; but it is a discipline of faith that will bring us into a knowledge of God which would otherwise be impossible.

". . . Satan has asked to sift you as wheat. But I have prayed for you . . . that your faith may not fail . . ." (Luke 22:31–32).

Paul said, "I have kept the faith," but he lost his head! They cut that off, but it didn't touch his faith. He rejoiced in three things—he had "fought the good fight," he had "finished the race," he had "kept the faith." What did all the rest amount to? Paul won the race; he gained the prize; and he has not only the admiration of earth today, but the admiration of heaven. Why do we not act as if it paid to lose all for Christ? Why are we not loyal to truth as he was? Ah, we haven't his arithmetic. He counted differently from us. We count the things *gain* that he counted *loss*. We must have his faith, and keep it, if we would wear the same crown.

DAY TWENTY-SIX

Commit your way to the Lord; trust in him and he will do this: He will make your righteousness shine like the dawn, the justice of your cause like the noonday sun (Ps. 37:5–6).

The word *trust* is the heart word of faith. It is the Old Testament word, the word given to the early and infant stage of faith. The word faith expresses more the act of the will, the word belief the act of the mind or intellect, but trust is the language of the heart. The other has reference more to a truth believed or a thing expected.

Trust implies more than this, it sees and feels, and leans upon a person, a great, true, living heart of love. So let us "trust in him," through all the delays, in spite of all the difficulties, in the face of all the denials, notwithstanding all the seemings, even when we cannot understand the way, and know not the issue; still "trust in him and he will do this." The way will open, the right issue will come, the end will be peace, the cloud will be lifted, and the light of an eternal noonday shall shine at last.

> Trust and rest when all around thee
> Puts thy faith to sorest test;
> Let no fear or foe confound thee,
> Wait for God and trust and rest.
>
> Trust and rest with heart abiding,
> Like a birdling in its nest,
> Underneath His feathers hiding,
> Fold thy wings and trust and rest.

His wife said to him, ". . . Curse God and die!" He replied, ". . . Shall we accept good from God, and not trouble?" (Job 2:9–10).

God's Divine goodness is not emptied out in heaps at our feet when we first start in faith's pathway; rather it is kept in reserve for us until we need it, and is then disbursed. Job knew this truth. He knew the Divine method, both in providence and in grace. He committed his family, his belongings, his very body to God. Though all was taken away from him, he trusted God and "the Lord made him prosperous again and gave him twice as much as he had before" (Job 42:10).

Still today there are those who say, "Silly one—to worship Christ!" There is only one answer to that jeer—to put your trust in God so deeply that every thought, every hope, every day of your living banks on Him, rests upon Him alone. There is only one answer that can be heard above the tumult of the world—your life, made victorious over all pain and heartbreak, because it rests upon the Rock of the Almighty.

"Come to me, all you who are weary and burdened, and I will give you rest. Take my yoke upon you and learn from me, for I am gentle and humble in heart, and you will find rest for your souls. For my yoke is easy and my burden is light" (Matt. 11:28–30).

Oh, the burdens that we love to bear and cannot understand! Oh, the inarticulate outreachings of our hearts for things we cannot comprehend! And yet we know they are an echo from the throne and a whisper from the heart of God. It is often a groan rather than a song, a burden rather than a buoyant wing. But it is a blessed burden, and it is a groan whose undertone is praise and unutterable joy. It is "a groaning which cannot be uttered." This is the deep mystery of prayer. This is the delicate divine mechanism which words cannot explain, but which the humblest believer knows even when he does not understand.

God never meant any man to carry the past and the future on his back, in addition to the tasks of today. You can straighten your back, and carry your hopes with assurance. The Lord bids us to take His yoke upon us. In other words, find out from Him what He wants you to carry, those responsibilities which He has chosen for you to bear. Then carry those, and forget all the needless burdens you have added yourself. Carry God's load for love of Him and of others. Carry it, trusting His wisdom in giving you that particular load. You will, like all honest men before you, make the surprising discovery that God always gives sufficient strength to carry the load He has appointed for you. It is as simple as that, "For my yoke is easy, and my burden is light."

We live by faith, not by sight (2 Cor. 5:7).

By faith, not sight; God never wants us to look at our feelings. Self may want us to; and Satan may want us to. But God wants us to face facts, not feelings; the facts of Christ and of His finished and perfect work for us.

When we face these precious facts, and believe them because God says they are facts, God will take care of our feelings.

God never gives feeling to enable us to trust Him; God never gives feeling to encourage us to trust Him; God never gives feeling to show that we have already and utterly trusted Him.

God gives feeling only when He sees that we trust Him apart from all feeling, resting on His own Word, and on His own faithfulness to His promise.

Never until then can the feeling (which is from God) possibly come; and God will give the feeling in such a measure and at such a time as His love sees best for the individual case.

We must choose between facing toward our feelings and facing toward God's facts. Our feelings may be as uncertain as the sea or the shifting sands. God's facts are as certain as the Rock of Ages, even Christ Himself, who is the same yesterday, today and forever.

> When darkness veils His lovely face
> I rest on His unchanging grace;
> In every high and stormy gale,
> My anchor holds within the veil.

Look to the Lord and his strength; seek his face always (Ps. 105:4).

On a day in the autumn, I saw a prairie eagle mortally wounded by a rifle shot. His eye still gleamed like a circle of light. Then he slowly turned his head, and gave one more searching and longing look at the sky. He had often swept those starry spaces with his wonderful wings. The beautiful sky was the home of his heart. It was the eagle's domain. A thousand times he had exploited there his splendid strength. In those far away heights he had played with the lightnings, and raced with the winds, and now, so far away from home, the eagle lay dying, done to the death, because for once he forgot and flew too low. The soul is that eagle. This is not its home. It must not lose the skyward look. We must keep faith, we must keep hope, we must keep courage, we must keep Christ. We would better creep away from the battlefield at once if we are not going to be brave. There is no time for the soul to stampede. Keep the skyward look, my soul; keep the skyward look!

> Keep looking up—
> The waves that roar around thy feet,
> Jehovah-Jireh will defeat
> When looking up.

Part 4

Winter

He says to the snow,
    "Fall on the earth,"
and to the rain shower,
    "Be a mighty downpour."
So that all men he has made
    may know his work,
he stops every man
    from his labor.

Job 37:6–7

Though an army besiege me, my heart will not fear; though war break out against me, even then will I be confident (Ps. 27:3).

Take away faith, and in vain we call to God. There is no other road betwixt our souls and heaven. Blockade that road and we cannot communicate with the Great King. Faith links us with Divinity.

An outstanding minister said that one evening he found himself staggering along under a load that was heavy enough to crush half a dozen strong men. Out of sheer exhaustion he put it down and took a good look at it. He found that it was all borrowed. Part of it belonged to the following day; part of it belonged to the following week, and here he was borrowing it that it might crush him *now*—a very stupid but a very ancient blunder.

Never yield to gloomy anticipations. Who told you that the night would never end in day? Who told you that the winter of your discontent should proceed from frost to frost, from snow and ice and hail to deeper snow? Do you not know that day follows night, that flood comes after the ebb, that spring and summer succeed winter? Place your hope and confidence in God. He has no record of failure.

DAY TWO

Be still before the Lord and wait patiently for him . . . (Ps. 37:7).

D r. Griffiths has written, "Quietness is not only the opposite of noise. It is the absence of excitement, haste, and consequent confusion. These dissipate strength, while calmness and deliberateness conserve it. The world's mighty men have grown in solitude. The prince of lawgivers and leader of Israel spent forty years in the wilderness and obscurity of Midian; the forerunner and pathmaker of our Lord found the flame of his forgiveness upon his lips and a 'Here am I, Lord.' Christ Himself faced the great questions involved in His ministry in quiet solitude. The zeal of Saint Paul sprang from the silence of Arabia. The vision of John was born in banishment. Peter, the hermit, aroused Europe to undertake the Crusades. Luther, the retiring monk, turned the current of history into a new civilization. Lincoln, the emancipator, came out of quiet mountains in Kentucky and vast forests in Illinois. Solitude—periods of quietness gave these heroes a chance to know self, nature, and God, and fitted them for their great service."

The silence beckons us. Learn the "art of stillness." It is safety, solace, strength. With this armament we overcome the noisesome pestilence.

Great is our Lord and mighty in power; his understanding has no limit (Ps. 147:5).

"he Infinite cannot be defined. There is no adequate definition of God. To define is to set limits, establish boundaries. God is boundless. God cannot be classified. Classification calls for similars and equals. God is transcendent, supreme."

—Unknown

In May and early June of 1940, 335,000 men were trapped on the sands of Dunkirk. It looked as though they would be wiped from the face of the earth. German land, air and naval fire beat the shores with merciless intensity and precision. They were surrounded and all that was left was a little sandy beach. It did not seem that all the powers of earth and heaven could ever rescue these men. Death seemed certain, but God sent a fog. The fog became thicker and thicker, and it lay over the evacuation area like a dense blanket until all the men were saved.

"After all, there is God!" He has His sun. He has the snow. He has the fog. He has the wind. He is the Master of every circumstance."

DAY FOUR

"I have learned to be content whatever the circumstances" (Phil. 4:11).

Paul, denied of every comfort, wrote the above words in his dungeon. A story is told of a king who went into his garden one morning, and found everything withered and dying. He asked the oak that stood near the gate what the trouble was. He found it was sick of life and determined to die because it was not tall and beautiful like the pine. The pine was all out of heart because it could not bear grapes, like the vine. The vine was going to throw its life away because it could not stand erect and have as fine fruit as the peach tree. The geranium was fretting because it was not tall and fragrant like the lilac; and so on all through the garden. Coming to a heart's-ease, he found its bright face lifted as cheery as ever. "Well, heart's-ease, I'm glad amidst all this discouragement, to find one brave little flower. You do not seem to be the least disheartened." "No, I am not of much account, but I thought that if you wanted an oak, or a pine, or a peach tree, or a lilac, you would have planted one; but as I knew you wanted a heart's-ease, I am determined to be the best little heart's-ease that I can."

> Others may do a greater work,
>   But you have your part to do;
> And no one in all God's heritage
>   Can do it so well as you.

They who are God's without reserve, are in every state content; for they will only what He wills, and desire to do for Him whatever He desires them to do; they strip themselves of everything, and in this nakedness find all things restored an hundredfold.

"Heaven and earth will pass away, but my words will never pass away" (Matt. 24:35).

Priscilla Howe once described the Word of God as the Book that contains the mind of God, the state of man, the way of salvation, the doom of sinners, and the happiness of believers. Its doctrines are holy, its precepts are binding, its histories are true, and its decisions are immutable. Therefore, how can it ever fade from the grasp of man? Read it to be wise, believe it to be safe, and practice it to be holy.

It contains light to direct you, food to support you, and comfort to cheer you. It is the traveler's map, the pilgrim's staff, the soldier's sword, and the Christian's charter. Here paradise is restored, heaven opened, and the gates of hell disclosed.

Christ is its grand object, our good its design, and the glory of God its end. It should fill the memory, rule the heart, and guide the feet. Read it slowly, frequently and prayerfully. It is a mine of wealth, a paradise of glory, and a river of pleasure.

It is given you in life, will be opened in the judgment, and be remembered forever. It involves the highest responsibility, will reward the greatest labor, and will condemn all who trifle with its sacred content.

The memory of the righteous will be a blessing . . . (Prov. 10:7).

A pear tree was overheard in my garden sighing to itself, shuddering in the cold November wind. "To what end is summer, if it must go away so soon? Why have I basked in the blessed sunshine, and drunk the evening dews, if now I am to be left by them both to the bitterness of this wintry desolation?" And it writhed and moaned in the agony of the storm. An ancient apple tree nearby replied, "You have forgotten that you have helped beautify the garden with the luxuriance of your foliage; that you have sweetened the air with the odor of your blossoms; that you have gladdened the household by the lusciousness of your fruits; that children have played under your shade; and, more than all, that you have grown, and that you still retain the gift of the summer in full six inches of length of bough, by which amount you are nearer the sky, stronger to bear the storm, readier to meet the coming of another spring, and fitter to enter on its new career with advantage."

Dear ones may be gone, but "the influence of the summer of their lives" is left upon us. Our hearts are warmer blessed and of use to others because of the benefits received from them. We can rest in their shadow and be the "better fitted for spring of immortality, where the sun shall never go down."

What a comforting promise was bestowed by Jesus when He left the fellowship of friends and loved ones of this earth. "I go to prepare a place for you." He was speaking to His followers of all generations and wanted them to be content that it was He who prepared it. Therefore, the fettered imagination can only anticipate what that place will be like. A writer aptly expressed his thinking when he said: "Its glory will surprise the rising of the sun, when that orb comes up with trembling shafts of light, through filmy curtains of clouds, and fills the eastern sky with opalescent splendors."

Find rest, O my soul, in God alone; my hope comes from him (Ps. 62:5).

Hope—what a precious word! How often have the Lord's dear children turned to the Psalms when perplexed and heavily laden and found just the right word to give strength, heartease and encouragement!

Commentators and reporters today have recently been giving to the nation some alarming facts of the present-day world conditions. Through the medium of television one catches a glimpse of world leaders sitting in their peace conferences and at the United Nations seeking some satisfactory way out of the chaotic and hopeless condition. What is to be gained by crying "Peace! Peace!" when there is no peace? Mankind already exists amid the ruins of a world full of broken homes, broken hopes, and broken hearts. One wonders no longer how true is the statement, "The world has gone to pieces." Man and all his wisdom, devices, and schemes will not solve the present-day problems. Look up, dear heart. There is a way out—but *one* way—and that way is God's way!

The wonderful apostle of faith, George Mueller, has left this testimony: "There is never a time when we may not *hope in God!* Whatever the necessities, however great our difficulties, and though to all appearances help is impossible, yet our business is to *hope in God,* and it will be found that it is not in vain."

DAY EIGHT

"If a man dies, will he live again? All the days of my hard service I will wait for my renewal to come" (Job 14:14).

There are men in ages past who have little more than their names recorded in the Holy Word. Yet they fulfilled a position at an appointed time for furthering the work of the Lord. Simeon, mentioned in Luke 2, was such a man. He waited his entire lifetime for just the one appointed task. He waited for the Messiah, and knew that he had not waited in vain.

Scientists tell us how the flowers of the alps are buried for long months under the snow, yet all the time they are full of energy and expectation. No sooner does the sunshine labor a few hours melting the snow than they open into glorious bloom. So aged Simeon waited through a long life, waited as beneath cold snows, but at the first kiss of the Sun of Righteousness he broke into flower and was accepted for one glorious responsibility—that of prophesying the work of salvation through the Babe he blessed in his arms.

My times are in your hands . . . (Ps. 31:15).

Many years ago a memorable dinner was given in London by Christopher Neville in honor of some of the leaders of English thought. They were leaders in politics, art, literature, finance and religion. For the after-dinner speeches Dean Stanley was asked to preside. No set address, and no topics were assigned. Upon arising the Dean proposed for discussion the question, "Who will dominate the future?" The first speaker he called upon was Professor Huxley. After a little skirmishing, Huxley gave as his thought that the future will be dominated by the nation that sticks most closely to the facts. He left his audience profoundly impressed. The Dean arose, after a moment of silence, and called upon an English writer, who was a member of Parliament as well as president of the Royal Commission of Education. Quietly he began by saying, "Gentlemen, I have been listening to the last speaker with profound interest and agree with him. I believe the future will belong to the nation that sticks to the facts. But I want to add one word—*all the facts,* not some of them, *all* of them. Now the greatest fact of history," he went on, "is God." GOD is the answer!

That dinner party in London is an event of the past, but the question, "Who shall dominate the future?" is still with us today in an aggravated form. The darkest days are just before the dawn.

"You, O Lord, keep my lamp burning; my God turns my darkness into light" (Ps. 18:28).

The Lord is good to those whose hope is in him, to the one who seeks him; it is good to wait quietly for the salvation of the Lord (Lam. 3:25–26).

It was the hour when defeat seemed inevitable that Joshua stood alone in prayer to God, and the answer was a glorious victory over the five kings.

It was the hours Elijah communed with God that brought fire from the sky which convinced Ahab that the Lord was God. It was the hours Jonah spent with Him in the deep sea when in the belly of the whale that prepared him to preach repentance to the people of Nineveh. It was the hours Daniel spent in the upper chamber alone with God that made him a prince among men, and also saved him in the den of lions. It was the hours the disciples spent in the upper room waiting upon the Lord which enabled them to preach three thousand souls into the Kingdom at Pentecost. It was the hours the Apostle Paul spent alone in prayer that enabled him to make Felix tremble and to make King Agrippa exclaim, "Almost thou persuadest me to be a Christian!" It was the hours Gladstone spent alone with God in prayer that made him the wise and safe leader of England. It was the hours Spurgeon spent alone in prayer that made him the greatest preacher since the days of Paul. It is the hours Billy Graham spends confiding in God that makes him the world's most influential revivalist today.

> I have a treasure which I prize,
>   Its like I cannot find;
> There's nothing like it on the earth—
>   'Tis this, a QUIET MIND.
> > —Unknown

And when he had said this, he showed them his hands and feet (Luke 24:40).

In the hands of Jesus there is certainty! There is providence! There is majesty! The hands of Jesus are human hands. They were once baby hands! Did not the angels from the realms of glory bid the shepherds to hasten to Bethlehem to behold those infant hands? For the fulness of time had come. The pagan empires had unknowingly set the stage. This great moment of which the prophets had spoken and the psalmists had sung had arrived! A body had been prepared for Him to permit the Godhead to be veiled in flesh.

In the course of time those tiny hands became toiling hands. He who fashioned the stars toiled in a carpenter's shed! His workmanship would be thorough. "We are His workmanship," cries Paul. He knew! Those hands that hewed rough timber into objects of beauty and usefulness had transformed him from a despot to a disciple, motivated not by law but by love.

The hands of Jesus are generous hands—generous in tender care. His hands were laid upon the little children in blessing when the stern disciples dared to drive them away.

His hands were generous in gifts of healing. Everywhere He went they brought unto Him all that were sick. His touch still has its ancient power.

His hands were generous in cleansing. He laid aside His robes and with His own hands He began to wash His disciples' feet. When Peter protested, Jesus replied, "Unless I wash you, you have no part with me" (John 13:8). Those hands are even today at our disposal when we need cleansing.

The hands of Jesus are saving hands. The Bible describes every type of sin but declares that the Lord delivers from them all.

His hands can save only because they are pierced hands.

The only things in heaven that man has made are the five wounds which are borne in His body. His wounded hands plead at the Throne of Grace for all who call upon the name of the Lord.

His saving hands are secure hands. Of all who come to Him He said, "I give them eternal life, and they shall never perish; no one can snatch them out of my hand" (John 10:28). They are able to hold secure for time and eternity all that we commit to Him.

Wait for the Lord; be strong and take heart and wait for the Lord (Ps. 27:14).

Wait for the Lord and keep his way. He will exalt you to possess the land . . . (Ps. 37:34).

Slow me down, Lord! Ease the pounding of my heart by the quieting of my mind. Steady my hurried pace with a vision of the eternal reach of time. Give me, amidst the confusion of my day, the calmness of the everlasting hills. Break the tensions of my nerves and muscles with the soothing music of the singing streams that live in my memory. Help me to know the magical, restoring power of sleep. Teach me the art of taking minute vacations . . . of slowing down to look at a flower, to chat with a friend, to pat a dog, to read a few lines from a good book. Remind me each day of the fable of the hare and the tortoise that I may know that the race is not always to the swift; that there is more to life than increasing its speed. Let me look upward into the branches of the towering oak and know that it grew great and strong because it grew slowly and well. Slow me down, Lord, and inspire me to send my roots deep into the soil of life's enduring values that I may grow toward the stars of my greater destiny. In Jesus' name, Amen."   —Unknown

We must learn to wait. When we do not know what to do we must simply do nothing. Wait till the fog clears away. Do not force a half-open door; a closed door may be providential.

There is grace supplied for the one who waits. The Psalmist knew this secret. He experienced this grace. "I wait for the Lord," he declared in Psalm 130:5. Waiting is a great part of life's discipline and therefore God often exercises the grace of waiting in the anxious hurrying person. "Waiting has four purposes," says Dr. James Vaughan. "It practices the patience of faith. It gives time for preparation for the coming gift. It makes the blessing the sweeter when it arrives. It shows the sovereignty of God—to give just *when* and *as* He pleases."

DAY THIRTEEN

Let not your heart be troubled; ye believe in God, believe also in Me. Let not your heart be troubled, neither let it be afraid (John 14:1, 27 KJV).

A soldier had returned home from the war and was telling about the grace of God which was with him. "A short time before I was wounded, I was invited by the officers of the regiment to a supper given in honour of a soldier who had been through all the war, and had done many brave deeds, but had received no reward for them. After the supper was over, one of the officers said to him, 'You have been through a lot, and you have not told us a single incident. Now tell us what you consider the most wonderful thing you have experienced in it.' He waited a moment, then replied, 'I was walking near my trench one day, when I saw a young soldier lying on the ground intently reading a book. I went up to him and asked him what he was reading. He told me it was the Bible. Now I had read the Bible for many years and it never did me any good. But this soldier said to me, "Listen to what I'm reading, 'Let not your heart be troubled ... In my Father's house are many mansions ... I go to prepare a place for you.'" He read on to the end of the chapter. "Oh, I have read that chapter many times! It never did me any good; give it up, man, give it up." He looked up at me and said, "If you knew what the Bible is to me, you'd never ask me to give it up," and, as he spoke, the light on his face was so bright, I never saw anything like it—it fairly dazzled me. I could not look at it, so I turned and walked away.

'Soon after a bomb fell near the place where we had been, and when the dust had cleared away I thought I'd go and see if that young soldier was safe. I found him fatally wounded, but I saw his Bible sticking out of his breast pocket, and here it is,' he said, holding it up. 'I say the most wonderful thing I have experienced during the war was the light on that young soldier's face, and more than that, I can now say that his Saviour is my Saviour too!'"

"Come to me, all you who are weary and burdened, and I will give you rest" (Matt. 11:28).

The secret of resting has been lost, and many are succumbing to the strain of life lived in "high gear." Rest is not a sedative for the sick, but a tonic for the strong. It spells emancipation, illumination, transformation! It saves us from becoming slaves, even of good works.

"See that your clock does not run down!" is the timely admonition sung by the colored people of the south. In my possession is an eight-day clock. One night after an unusually strenuous day, when the physical was taxed to the uttermost, and we had forgotten the place where "the flocks rested at noon," we found ourselves carrying loads that belonged to the next day, the next month, the next year. Sleep wanted to take its departure—we listened to the slow and very feeble tick of this clock, and it seemed to say, "I am all run down and cannot go on much longer." It was growing fainter and fainter, and shortly would have stopped had not a voice from the adjoining room called out, "the clock is running down; someone had better get up and wind it before it stops." And, someone obeyed! After a few moments we listened, we heard again the strong, steady, tick, tick, tick. The clock had been wound and this was the result. A still, small voice spoke to my inner heart, and the haunting refrain of the Negro spiritual, "See that your clock does not run down," hummed itself into the deepest recesses of my being.

And I saw that all labor and all achievement spring from man's envy of his neighbor. This too is meaningless, a chasing after the wind (Eccl. 4:4).

There is a time for everything and a season for every activity under heaven (Eccl. 3:1).

radition tells us that one day a hunter found the Apostle John seated on the ground playing with a tame quail. The hunter expressed his surprise that a man so earnest should be spending his time so profitlessly. John looked up and asked, "Why is the bow on your shoulder unstrung?" To this the hunter replied, "If kept always taut, it would lose its spring." The kindly apostle said with a smile, "For the same reason I play with this bird."

We must know how to put occupation aside. In an inaction which is meditative, the wrinkles of the soul are smoothed away.

It is not possible for many to have holidays and vacations at seashores or in mountain glens. We are a busy folk, and we must learn the blessed secret of resting just where we are.

Unless a kernel of wheat falls to the ground and dies, it remains only a single seed. But if it dies, it produces many seeds (John 12:24).

Can we expect a revival ere the Lord's return? Is the world so war-minded that we need not pray for revival until conditions are better?

Charles G. Finney said, "Would you have an awakening in your community, your church, your own lives; then become the fuel, and a revival fire will be the result."

The cost is high. Death to sin and self is the only roadway to power. Will we become God's fuel in bringing this to pass? Let us give the answer to God in some quiet place today as we covenant to wait upon Him until He has flooded our own souls with Himself.

Lord, send a revival! Begin it today!

> Revive us, Lord! Is zeal abating
>   While harvest fields are vast and white?
> Revive us, Lord! The world is waiting;
>   Equip Thy Church to send the Light.
>
> When naught whereon to lean remaineth,
>   When strongholds crumble to the dust,
> When nothing's sure but that God reigneth,
>   That, yes, that is the time to trust.
>
> —Author Unknown

DAY SEVENTEEN

The sacrifices of God are a broken spirit; a broken and contrite heart, O God, you will not despise (Ps. 51:17).

A shattered and broken personality releases the fragrance of Christ. Jacob was broken at Peniel when he wrestled with God. Mary was broken at Bethany when Lazarus was taken from her.

Why must it be a broken personality? Is it not wholeness of character that we have always heard about that gives off the perfume of holiness? The word wholeness is connected with holiness and health—spiritual health. We know that wholeness without God means danger and finally failure.

An illustration is given regarding broken personality. James McConkey purposed to be a lawyer, and spent years training for the bar. Family bereavement led him to combine his study with his business. It was too much for him. Though he reached his desired goal, he broke under the strain. In his breaking God brought him into the life of full surrender, reflecting the glory of God. He had written many meditations and thoughts for those who needed encouragement and strength. In his *God Planned Life* he uses this illustration: A beautiful, very beautiful stained-glass window in a cathedral was the object of attraction to many tourists. One night an awful storm raged; the whole window frame blew in, and the glass smashed in atoms on the floor. The sorrowful people of the city gathered up the fragments, placed them in a box and removed them to the crypt. One day a stranger came, and asked permission to see them and if he might take them away. "Yes," they said, "we have no use for them." Later came a mysterious invitation to some of those city authorities from a well-known artist in stained glass. A curtain was removed in his studio, and there was their beautiful window, only more, *much more beautiful* than before—a gift from the artist to take home.

"For I know that through your prayers and the help given by the Spirit of Jesus Christ, what has happened to me will turn out for my deliverance" (Phil. 1:19).

hat an opportunity to be able to look into a strong man's life and examine his resources. That is our privilege with St. Paul the Apostle, the greatest itinerant missionary. He found a gracious part of his resources in the prayers of others. Thus, we see that a person with one talent can be the invisible help-meet of the man with ten.

What was the occasion that so desperately required the faithful to be in prayer? Paul was in bonds! He had covered vast areas on enterprising ventures for the cause of the kingdom of God. He had passed through Asia Minor, remote lands, icy-cold mountains, fever-haunted plains. Genial fires had been kindled by God's torch-bearer for the "Kingdom of Light." Now the great missionary Paul was a captive. His torch seemingly was to be blown out. Not Paul! His chain was proof of his faith—a witness of a nobler freedom. Now was the time for another to battle for him and reap a conquest. How? By putting to use the greatest force in the known world. By prayer the powers of great men and women can be liberated and make them mighty masters of difficult circumstances.

One can travel through foreign fields with missionaries and can help them to be light-hearted in the midst of appalling tasks. The preacher needs a companion when he stands in the pulpit. His resources need to be multiplied when he proclaims the Word of Life. Yes, there are many who can make conquests in the league of prayer. In this way Onesimus was a part of Paul. Aquila was a part of Apollos. And any Christian can be a part of any great "kingdom" warrior in the field of life.

Prayer by those at home-base is the appointed means by which God's arm of love reaches out to the crying needs of His servants. Therefore, vital prayer is not just a word—it is an act!

DAY NINETEEN

*Remember all thy offerings, and accept thy burnt sacrifice (Ps. 20:3
KJV).*

While I was visiting the lovely Redwoods of California, one grand old Sequoia brought a new revelation into my heart. This was the place where live the giants—some over three hundred feet in height. Imagine what it would be like to actually see something living today that was alive when our Lord walked the earth! Walking among these trees you can gaze upon and even touch those who shared the age of Abraham! Astounding as it is, this was not the revelation.

One day a thoughtless person had dropped a lighted match near the foot of an ancient sentinel, which had stood for centuries guarding the forest, deepening its roots, expanding its height. A slow steady fire continued for three long years until gradually it burned the heart out, leaving but a reddish-brown wrinkled shell. To passersby it appeared as any of the other gigantic Redwoods. But one can enter its base and look up through the top and view the starry heavens. Amazing, but this was not the secret revealed.

What was the result of its devastation? The heart's ashes had become the impregnator for seven new young giants to sprout around that old dead base. Many are the hard cold winters of snow and wind on these mountains. (The tallest mountain peak in the Continental United States is here.) Storms have sought to uproot them, but "the wind that blows can never kill the tree God plants."

That morning we found a secret sanctuary, and turning to God's Word we read in Psalm 20:3, margin, these words: "Turn to ashes my burnt offering." Life comes out of death! This was the revelation! If there is no death, there is no resurrection!

Is the price for fruitage too great?

. . . neither height nor depth, nor anything else in all creation, will be able to separate us from the love of God that is in Christ Jesus our Lord (Rom. 8:39).

Such wondrous love!

What is there about the cross of Christ that gives it such great power and unwaning glory? From earliest history the cross has been known as the "accursed tree"—an instrument of torture, a place of punishment for the most hardened and wicked criminals—a mark of deepest shame and disgrace. But since the time of Christ, the cross adorns great cathedrals and beautiful altars. Throughout Christendom it is the symbol of all that is true and holy, all that is noble and merciful and loving. If we understand this, we know why the cross "towers o'er the wrecks of time."

The cross symbolizes God's great love for us. It is not an accident or a tragedy, but the universal sign of God's love for sinful man. The cross is the only adequate explanation of John 3:16. Our Father was not compelled to permit the cross; His love for us constrained Him. Willingly Christ gave His life because He loved us and desired us to live with Him in His eternal kingdom. "Greater love has no one than this, that one lay down his life for his friends" (John 15:13).

"Out from the ivory palaces into the world of woe" came the One who was sent—the One who delighted in doing His Father's will. They called His name Jesus.

> Under an Eastern sky
> Amid the rabble cry,
> A man went forth to die
>   For me!
>
> Thorn-crowned His blessed head,
> Blood-stained His every tread.
> To Calvary He was Led
>   For me!

Love led Him to Calvary. Love costs!

"If anyone would come after me, he must deny himself and take up his cross daily and follow me. For whoever wants to save his life will lose it, but whoever loses his life for me will save it" (Luke 9:23–24).

From somewhere out of the past came the Greatest Story Ever Told of the Greatest Life Ever Lived. From whence came the Book of all books, the Lamp of our feet, the Light for our path as we travel along earth's dark roads? How did it reach you—reach me?

God's will and His plan was made known to those who were willing to lose their lives that the story of Calvary love might reach every creature. He found those to whom He could commit sacred costs—men who were willing to be hidden away in underground dungeons, lay their heads upon martyr's blocks, and die for the cause. Because they were not disobedient to the heavenly vision, God's precious Word has been printed in more than a thousand languages. Today, faithful servants of His are busily engaged in the translation of other thousands of tribal tongues. What a debt of gratitude we owe to these honored heroes of the Cross.

It costs to carry the message. "Unless a kernel of wheat falls to the ground and dies, it remains only a single seed," were the words spoken by the Holy Spirit to a humble servant of His who had, after a day of heavy toil, gone aside into a quiet room to spend a night in prayer. What followed that trysting time with his Master during the brief hours of that night? What had happened that so completely changed his life thereafter? He had met Someone! To the one known throughout missionary circles as "the Missionary-Warrior"—Charles E. Cowman—had come a revelation of God's will that every home in an entire nation was to receive a portion of the sacred Scriptures, that a personal invitation was to be given to everyone living within that nation. That the time for such a crusade was now. When God says "today" He does not mean "tomorrow."

The challenge was accepted and in the name of the God of the Impossible, action began—for action ever follows vision.

During the following five years the greatest gospel distribution Crusade since Pentecost was launched when 10,320,000 homes in the Mikado's empire were visited personally and given portions of the precious old Book we so love. Thousands destroyed their idols and accepted the invitation of the One who said, "Come unto Me."

DAY TWENTY-TWO

. . . at his appointed season he brought his work to light through the preaching entrusted to me by the command of God, our Savior . . . (Titus 1:3).

There is some great hope, some burning desire, to serve your Lord? There are places to go and precious persons to reach before it is too late? You must needs be up and doing *now*? Earnestly you seek the will of God. "Where shall it be, dear Lord? When is the time? How shall I prepare?" You fear you may miss the sweet whisperings of God! Before you take the first step, dear worker, you must have constant assurance that He is guiding, that your Father is at the helm of your ship on the sea of life.

"Tell the Israelites to move on" (Exod. 14:15). This unrepealed charge of Jehovah rings down the ages to all children of faith. When all outward circumstances say that it is impossible to go forward, then it is God's time to do it. When it requires a miracle to go forward, that is God's time.

O, for grace to wait and watch for God! His "set time" will come. "Ye have need of patience." Answers to prayer are delayed at times for the strengthening of our confidence in God. Abraham waited twenty-five years for the answer to the promise that a son would be given him. Daniel waited twenty days for the answer to a petition for the interpretation of a vision. The sisters of Lazarus waited some days for Jesus to answer their request concerning their brother and He answered it in such a different manner from that they had expected.

God's set time will come. It will come quietly and gently as a sunbeam stealing through an open window on a summer's morn and a precious experience is ours that will be ours forever.

> In the second month the peachtree blooms,
> But not until the ninth the chrysanthemums—
> So each must wait till his own time comes.
> —Japanese Proverb

So Jacob was left alone, and a man wrestled with him till daybreak (Gen. 32:24).

Left alone! What different sensations those words conjure up to each of us. To some they spell loneliness and desolation, to others rest and quiet. To be left alone *without* God, would be too awful for words, but to be left alone *with* Him is a foretaste of heaven! If His followers spent more time alone with Him, we should have spiritual giants again.

The Master set us an example. Note how often He went to be *alone with God;* and He had a mighty purpose behind the command, "When you pray, go into your room, close the door and pray to your Father, who is unseen" (Matt. 6:6).

The greatest miracles of Elijah and Elisha took place when they were alone with God. It was alone with God that Jacob became a prince. Joshua was alone when the Lord came to him (Josh. 1:1). Gideon and Jephthah were by themselves when commissioned to save Israel (Judg. 6:11; 11:29). Moses was by himself at the wilderness bush (Exod. 3:1–5). Cornelius was praying by himself when the angel came to him (Acts 10:2). No one was with Peter on the house top when he was instructed to go to the Gentiles (Acts 10:9). John the Baptist was alone in the wilderness (Luke 1:80), and John the Beloved alone in Patmos, when nearest God (Rev. 1:9).

Covet to get alone with God. If we neglect it, we not only rob ourselves, but others too, of blessing, since when we are blessed we are able to pass on blessing to others. It may mean less outside work; it must mean more depth and power, and the consequence, too, will be "they saw no man save Jesus only."

To be alone with God in prayer cannot be over-emphasized.

DAY TWENTY-FOUR

Blessed are those whose strength is in you. . . . As they pass through the Valley . . . they make it a place of springs (Ps. 84:5–6).

Comfort does not come to the light-hearted and merry. We must go down into "depths" if we would experience this most precious of God's gifts—comfort, and thus be prepared to be co-workers together with Him.

When night—needful night—gathers over the garden of our souls, when the leaves close up, and the flowers no longer hold any sunlight within their folded petals, there shall never be wanting, even in the thickest darkness, drops of heavenly dew—dew which falls only when the sun has gone.

I have been through the valley of weeping,
    The valley of sorrow and pain;
But the "God of all comfort" was with me,
    At hand to uphold and sustain.

As the earth needs the clouds and sunshine,
    Our souls need both sorrow and joy;
So He places us oft in the furnace,
    The dross from the gold to destroy.

When He leads thro' some valley of trouble,
    His omnipotent hand we trace;
For the trials and sorrows He sends us,
    Are part of His lessons in grace.

Oft we shrink from the purging and pruning,
    Forgetting the Husbandman knows
That the deeper the cutting and paring,
    The richer the cluster that grows.

Well He knows that affliction is needed;
    He has a wise purpose in view,
And in the dark valley He whispers,
    "Hereafter Thou'lt know what I do."

As we travel thro' life's shadow'd valley,
  Fresh springs of His love ever rise;
And we learn that our sorrows and losses,
  Are blessings just sent in disguise.

So we'll follow wherever He leadeth,
  Let the path be dreary or bright;
For we've proved that our God can give comfort;
  Our God can give songs in the night.

"You will leave me all alone. Yet I am not alone, for my Father is with me" (John 16:32).

I t need not be said that to carry out conviction into action is a costly sacrifice. It may make necessary renunciations and separations which leave one to feel a strange sense both of deprivation and loneliness. But he who will fly, as an eagle does, into the higher levels where cloudless day abides, and live in the sunshine of God, must be content to live a comparatively lonely life.

No bird is so solitary as the eagle. Eagles never fly in flocks; one, or at most two, ever being seen at once. But the life that is lived unto God, however it forfeits human companionships, *knows Divine fellowship.*

God seeks eagle-men. No man ever comes into a realization of the best things of God, who does not, upon the God-ward side of his life, learn to walk alone with God. We find Abraham alone in Horeb upon the heights, but Lot dwelling in Sodom. Moses, skilled in all the wisdom of Egypt must go forty years into the desert alone with God. Paul, who was filled with Greek learning and had also sat at the feet of Gamaliel, must go into Arabia and learn the desert life with God. Let God isolate us. I do not mean the isolation of a monastery. In this isolating experience He develops an independence of faith and life so that the soul needs no longer the constant help, prayer, faith or attention of his neighbor. Such assistance and inspiration from the other members are necessary and have their place in the Christian's development, but there comes a time when they act as a direct hindrance to the individual's faith and welfare. God knows how to change the circumstances in order to give us an isolating experience. We yield to God and He takes us through something, and when it is over, those about us, who are no less loved than before, are no longer depended upon. We realize that He has wrought some things in us, and that the wings of our souls have learned to beat the upper air.

We must dare to be alone. Jacob must be left alone if the Angel of God is to whisper in his ear the mystic name of Shiloh; Daniel must be left alone if he is to see celestial visions; John must be banished to Patmos if he is deeply to take and firmly to keep "the print of heaven."

He trod the wine-press alone. Are we prepared for a "splendid isolation" rather than fail Him?

Now Isaac . . . went out to the field one evening to meditate . . .
(Gen. 24:62–63).

W̲e should be better Christians if we were more alone; we should do more if we attempted less, and spent more time in retirement, and quiet waiting upon God. The world is too much with us; we are afflicted with the idea that we are doing nothing unless we are fussily running to and fro; we do not believe in "the calm retreat, the silent shade." As a people, we are of a very practical turn of mind; "we believe," as someone has said, "in having all our irons in the fire, and consider the time not spent between the anvil and the fire as lost, or much the same as lost." Yet no time is more profitably spent than that which is set apart for quiet musing, for talking with God, for looking up to heaven. We cannot have too many of these open spaces in life, hours in which the soul is left accessible to any sweet thought or influence it may please God to send.

Let us often in these days give our mind a "Sunday," in which it will do no manner of work but simply lie still, and look upward, and spread itself out before the Lord like Gideon's fleece, to be soaked and moistened with the dews of heaven. Let there be intervals when we shall do nothing, think nothing, plan nothing, but just lay ourselves on the green lap of nature and "rest awhile."

Time so spent is not lost time. The fisherman cannot be said to be losing time when he is mending his nets, nor the mower when he takes a few minutes to sharpen his scythe at the top of the ridge. City men cannot do better than follow the example of Isaac, and, as often as they can, get away from the fret and fever of life. Wearied with the heat and din, the noise and bustle, communion with nature is very grateful; it will have a calming, healing influence. A walk through the fields, a saunter by the seashore or across the daisy-sprinkled meadows, will purge your life from sordidness, and make the heart beat with new joy and hope.

Mary Magdalene and the other Mary were sitting there across from the tomb (Matt. 27:61).

How strangely stupid is grief. It neither learns nor knows nor wishes to learn or know. When the sorrowing sisters sat over against the door of God's sepulchre, did they see the two thousand years that have passed triumphing away? Did they see anything but this: "Our Christ is gone!"

Your Christ and my Christ came from their loss; myriad mourning hearts have had resurrection in the midst of their grief; and yet the sorrowing watchers looked at the seed-form of this result, and saw nothing. What they regarded as the end of life was the very preparation for the coronation; for Christ was silent that He might live again in tenfold power.

They saw it not. They mourned, they wept, and went away, and came again, driven by their hearts to the sepulchre. Still it was a sepulchre, unprophetic, voiceless, lusterless.

So with us. Every man sits over against the sepulchre in his garden, in the first instance, and says, "This woe is irremediable. I see no benefit in it. I will take no comfort in it." And yet, right in our deepest and worst mishaps, often, our Christ is lying, waiting for resurrection.

Where our death seems to be, there our Saviour is. Where the end of hope is, there is the brightest beginning of fruition. Where the darkness is thickest, there the bright beaming light that never is set is about to emerge. When the whole experience is consummated, then we find that a garden is not disfigured by a sepulchre. Our joys are made better if there be sorrow in the midst of them. And our sorrows are made bright by the joys that God has planted around about them. The flowers may not be pleasing to us, they may not be such as we are fond of plucking, but they are heart-flowers, love, hope, faith, joy, peace—these are flowers which are planted around about every grave that is sunk in the Christian heart.

141

"Wait, my daughter, until you find out what happens. For the man will not rest until the matter is settled today" (Ruth 3:18).

Paradise has vanished from our world, as the picture of a landscape vanishes when swept by storm. And our race stands in much the same plight as did Naomi and Ruth in this old-world story. We have lost our inheritance, and the one barrier which stands between us and despair is the Person and Work of our Lord Jesus Christ. But, thank God, we need have no doubt as to the sequel. For as Boaz claimed back the estate for Ruth, so may we be confident that Jesus Christ will never be at rest till this sin-stained and distracted world is restored to her primitive order and beauty, as when the morning stars sang for joy.

Jesus is our near Kinsman by His assumption of our nature. He is the nearest and dearest Friend of our race, who stooped to die for our redemption. And the fact that He carried our nature in Himself to heaven, and wears it there, is an indissoluble bond between us. Sit still! Do not fret! He will never fail, as He will certainly never forsake!

Let us seek the quiet heart in our prayers. Prayer must arise within us as a fountain from unknown depths. But we must leave it to God to answer in His own wisest way. We are so impatient and think that God does not answer. A child asked God for fine weather on her birthday, and it rained! Someone said, "God didn't answer your prayer." "Oh, yes," she replied, "He did. God always answers, but He said No!" God always answers! He never fails! Be still! If we abide in Him, and He abides in us, we ask what we will, and it is done. As a sound may dislodge an avalanche, so the prayer of faith sets in motion the power of God.

"Be still, and know that I am God . . ." (Ps. 46:10).

All-loving Father, sometimes we have walked under starless skies that dripped darkness like drenching rain. We despaired of starshine or moonlight or sunrise. The sullen blackness gloomed above us as if it would last forever. And out of the dark there spoke no soothing voice to mend our broken hearts. We would gladly have welcomed some wild thunder peal to break the torturing stillness of that over-brooding night.

But Thy winsome whisper of eternal love spoke more sweetly to our bruised and bleeding souls than any winds that breathe across aeolian harps. It was Thy "still small voice" that spoke to us. We were listening and we heard. We looked and saw Thy face radiant with the light of love. And when we heard Thy voice and saw Thy face, new life came back to us as life comes back to withered blooms that drink the summer rain.

DAY THIRTY

"To him who sits on the throne and to the Lamb be praise and honor and glory and power, for ever and ever!" (Rev. 5:13).

The Alpine shepherds have a beautiful custom of ending the day by singing to one another an evening farewell.

The air is so crystalline that the song will carry long distances. As the dusk begins to fall, they gather their flocks and begin to lead them down the mountain paths, singing, "Hitherto hath the Lord helped us. Let us praise His name!"

And at last with a sweet courtesy, they sing to one another the friendly farewell: "Goodnight! Goodnight!" The words are taken up by the echoes, and from side to side the song goes reverberating sweetly and softly until the music dies away in the distance.

So let us call out to one another through the darkness, till the gloom becomes vocal with many voices, encouraging the pilgrim host. Let the echoes gather till a very storm of Hallelujahs breaks in thundering waves around the sapphire throne, and then as the morning breaks we shall find ourselves at the margin of the sea of glass, crying, with the redeemed host, "Blessing and honor and glory be unto him that sitteth on the throne and to the Lamb forever and ever!"